W9-AQI-999

A TEACHER'S

*Pocket
Guide to
School Law*

A TEACHER'S

Pocket Guide to School Law

Nathan L. Essex
Southwest Tennessee Community College
University of Memphis

Boston   New York   San Francisco
Mexico City   Montreal   Toronto   London
Madrid   Munich   Paris
Hong Kong   Singapore   Tokyo   Cape Town   Sydney

Senior Editor: Arnis E. Burvikovs
Series Editorial Assistant: Kelly Hopkins
Marketing Manager: Tara Kelly
Production Editor: Janet Domingo
Editorial Production Service: Lynda Griffiths
Composition Buyer: Andrew Turso
Manufacturing Buyer: Andrew Turso
Electronic Composition: PD & PS
Interior Design: PD & PS
Cover Administrator: Joel Gendron

For related titles and support materials, visit our online catalog at www.ablongman.com.

Between the time website information is gathered and then published, it is not unusual for some sites to have closed. Also, the transcription of URLs can result in typographical errors. The publisher would appreciate notification where these errors occur so that they may be corrected in subsequent editions.

ISBN: 0-205-45215-9

Printed in the United States of America

10 9 8 7 6 5 4 3 2 1   09 08 07 06 05

Dedicated to my spouse, Lorene,
and to my children,
Kimberly, Jarvis, and Nathalie

Contents

CHAPTER *three*
Religion and Public Schools   22

CHAPTER *four*
Students, the Law, and Public Schools   35

List of Cases

Preface

How do teachers respond to legal challenges they encounter as they perform their important duties of teaching, supervising, and protecting the safety of students under their supervision? How do they know that their actions are not depriving students of their constitutional rights? How can they be certain they are operating within the boundaries of the law? How do they demonstrate fundamental fairness in their dealings with students? *A Teacher's Pocket Guide to School Law* is based on the premise that public school teachers must be knowledgeable of the law that governs the organization and operation of schools in which they are employed.

Teachers as professionals will need to exercise discretion in rendering sound and legally defensible decisions that affect students under their care. Additionally, teachers must possess the basic legal knowledge necessary to successfully accomplish their important duties. The goal of this book is to provide comprehensive yet succinct and practical knowledge regarding relevant legal issues that impact teachers in public schools. This book includes a thorough discussion of the control of public schools and how it affects public school teachers. It proceeds with a brief reference to landmark court cases that have shaped administrative practices in public schools. Areas such as religion, student rights, teacher freedoms, student and faculty disabilities, tenure, dismissal, and Internet use are discussed, among other topics. One salient feature of this book is its focus on school safety and the due process rights of students in cases involving discipline. Discussion of topics is supported by tables and charts that are carefully integrated in the text to amplify concepts introduced for the reader. Pre-service teachers, in-service teachers, college and university teachers, education faculty, and supervisors, policymakers, and central office supervisors in public schools will gain valuable knowledge that will enable them to perform their respective duties efficiently and effectively within the boundaries of constitutional, statutory, and case law.

This book is free of legal jargon and organized and written in a style that facilitates ease of reading even for those who have little or no legal backgrounds. Legal citations are used to support and enhance the discussion of major legal issues. Legal references that support the topics under discussion are found throughout the book, thus enabling the reader to readily ascertain the legal source of authority related to those topics.

One unique feature of this book is its focus on the development of guides related to major issues discussed in each chapter. These guides provide readers pertinent information to direct their day-to-day decisions as they face a wide range of legal challenges within their schools. Finally, the book ends with appendices that include relevant constitutional provisions, carefully selected annotated federal statutes, and information on relevant educational resources. An abbreviated glossary of important legal terms is also enclosed to assist the reader and provide relevance to the body of the text.

A Teacher's Pocket Guide to School Law provides practical and useful resource guides for teachers and other school professionals to increase their knowledge and understanding of the complex legal issues affecting their organizations. This resource will enable professional educators to perform their legal duties more effectively and do so within the boundaries of the law.

ACKNOWLEDGMENTS

My sincere appreciation goes to my administrative secretary, Carol Brown, for the countless hours spent preparing this document. Her relentless energy, enthusiasm, encouragement, and support far exceeded my expectations. For her untiring efforts, I am eternally grateful.

For their helpful comments, thanks to the following reviewers: Sherion Jackson, Texas A&M Commerce; Michael Jacons, University of Northern Colorado; Mary K. McCullough, Loyola Marymount University; and Nancy H. Stankus, Shippensburg University of PA.

Thanks, too, to my family for their love, support, and encouragement during the writing of this text. Their support provided me inspiration to persevere through the completion of this project.

I convey my gratitude to Nathalie Essex, third-year law student at St. Louis University, for her expert editorial and technical assistance that helped me greatly in the production of this text.

Last, I express appreciation to my administrative team, friends, and colleagues for their support and encouragement during the writing of this book.

To my staff, colleagues, and family, I am immensely grateful.

About the Author

Nathan L. Essex is professor of Educational Administration in the College of Education at The University of Memphis and President of Southwest Tennessee Community College. He received the B.S. degree in English at Alabama A&M University, the M.S. degree in Educational Administration at Jacksonville State University, and the Ph.D. degree in Administration and Planning at The University of Alabama.

Essex's interests include law, educational policy, and personnel administration. He has served as consultant for more than 100 school districts and numerous educational agencies. He worked as a policy consultant with the Alabama State Department of Education for 12 years and received numerous awards in recognition of his contributions in the field of education. He is the recipient of the Truman M. Pierce Award for Educational Leadership, making outstanding contributions that advanced the direction of education in the state of Alabama, and the Academic Excellence Award in recognition of professional achievement and academic excellence. Other awards include those from the Capstone College of Education Society, The University of Alabama; Teaching Excellence Award, The University of Alabama; Distinguished Service Award—Who's Who in the State of Tennessee and The University of Memphis Distinguished Administrator of the Year 1995–96; and Alpha Beta Gamma's National Community College President of the Year—just to name a few.

Essex has published numerous articles, book chapters, and newsletters on legal issues. Many of his works appear in *The Administrator's Notebook, The Horizon, Compensation Review, The Clearinghouse, The American School Board Journal, Education and the Law, The School Administrator,* and many other professional journals. He is highly sought by educators at all levels to share his knowledge and expertise regarding legal issues that impact public schools.

Introduction

The United States is a nation grounded in law. Public schools operate within the boundaries of established law. Public school law covers a wide array of subject matter that directly affects the organization and administration of public schools. Consequently, school personnel must be knowledgeable of the law and its impact on the daily operation of schools. A significant body of law relates specifically to education, but an even greater body of law influences the operation of government. Since education is a function of state government, these laws directly affect public school systems.

Enacted law is derived from federal and state constitutions as well as federal and state statutes. Common law, or case law—the most prevalent source—is derived from court decisions. Judicial decisions play a significant role in the management and operation of public schools. Decisions by the courts frequently alter school district policies and practices. Therefore, it is incumbent on school personnel to be knowledgeable of the law and to operate within the parameters established by case law. For example, parental rights and responsibilities involving their children, tort liability, and essentials of contracts are based on common law doctrine.

It is interesting to note that law reflects the social and political patterns of society. Thus, court decisions should be examined in the context of the prevailing social and political climate that exists during the time in which the decision is rendered. Additionally, some courts are liberal and others are conservative in their rulings based on their composition. Added to this dynamic is the fact that law is an ever-changing field of study that requires school personnel to remain current in developments that affect the operation of schools.

Since school law is viewed as a generic field of study that covers a broad range of subject matter, it is vitally important that school personnel be well versed in the basic legal concepts supporting school law and be able to apply legal concepts to practices in public schools.

Chapter 1 provides the legal framework within which public schools operate and includes sources of law such as the federal and state constitutions, federal and state statutes, and the U.S. System of Courts. Emphasis is placed on the important role these sources play in shaping policies, rules, and regulations for the operation of public schools.

Chapter 2 covers instruction and curriculum issues as well as federal statutes that impact the instructional program. School vouchers and charter schools are also discussed, along with academic prerogatives involving teachers.

Chapter 3 addresses religion in public schools. It identifies religious issues that impact public schools with an emphasis on separation of church and state, the principle of neutrality, and the basic tenets of the First Amendment with respect to religious rights and freedoms of students.

Chapter 4 provides an overview of the constitutional rights of students in public schools and the relationship between school personnel and students with respect to student freedoms. Emphasis is placed on the reasonableness of school rules and regulations in relation to the personal rights and freedoms of students.

Chapter 5 includes a focused discussion of the due process rights of students in the context of establishing safe schools where teachers can teach and students can learn. Gang violence is discussed, including measures that school personnel may take to minimize violence in public schools.

Chapter 6 covers the privacy rights of students in public schools and their parents. Measures are discussed that are necessary to protect the confidentiality of student records as well as liability challenges involving defamation that may emerge when students' privacy rights are violated.

Chapter 7 addresses individuals with disabilities and the legal requirements that must be met regarding their educational needs. Relevant issues involving placement, related services, and the due process rights of students with disabilities and their parents are discussed.

Chapter 8 provides a discussion of school liability and teachers' duties to protect students from foreseeable harm. Defenses to liability are discussed as well as liability based on failure to meet the proper standard of care in instructing and supervising students.

Chapter 9 addresses discrimination in employment issues and the rights that are afforded teachers under the Fourteenth Amendment with respect to fairness in the employment process. Federal statutes are discussed that provide protection against employment discrimination in public schools.

Chapter 10 covers the rights and freedoms in which public school teachers are entitled in the school environment, along with reasonable restrictions that school officials may place on teachers under certain conditions.

Chapter 11 discusses teacher employment issues involving tenure, dismissal, and collective negotiations, along with the legal requirements that are necessary to protect teachers. Property rights regarding tenure and due process provisions are addressed, as well as liberty interests involving non-tenured teachers.

CHAPTER

one

Control of Public Schools

STATE AND LOCAL CONTROL OF EDUCATION

Public education is a federal interest, a state function, and a local responsibility. A federal interest is manifested through the passage of various federal statutes, such as Title I: Goals 2000, Educate America Act of 1994, Education for Disabled Students, and No Child Left Behind, that impact the operation of public schools. These statutes are aimed at improving the quality of public education and creating greater accountability for achieving desired educational outcomes. The Tenth Amendment to the U.S. Constitution provides that the powers not delegated to the United States by the Constitution nor prohibited by it to the states are reserved to the states respectively and to the people. Thus, by virtue of the Tenth Amendment, the control of education is vested in the states and the people. The responsibility for the operation and control of public schools resides with the state. Unless restricted by state constitutions, state legislatures have the authority to govern public schools. Most state constitutions make reference to the legislature's responsibility for public education. Although the state legislature has the ultimate control over public schools, its control is not unrestricted, but is subject to review by state and federal courts to ensure that the constitutional rights of citizens are protected.

The state legislature has plenary power to establish schools and develop a unique system of public schools. This legislative power was illustrated in a very early Michigan decision when the court held that the legislature has entire control over the schools of the state, the division of the territory of the states into districts, the conduct of the school, and the qualifications of teachers. The subjects to be taught therein are all within the state's control.[1] The power of the state to control education is derived from the state's police power, which means that the state is responsible for the health, safety, and welfare of its citizens. The police power of a state extends to the protection of the lives, limbs, health, comfort, and quiet of all persons and to the protection of all property within the state.[2] State legislatures have the authority to govern education involving both the legislative and executive branches of government, including regulations promotive of domestic order, morals, health, and safety.[3]

Children who enroll in public schools are subject to state laws and local regulations governing the operation of public schools. It is through the state's police powers that it has the authority to control education, including such matters as requiring compulsory attendance and immunization for children attending public schools. Since the state has police powers that allow it to exercise rules and regulations designed to protect the health, safety, and well-being of all citizens, it is also within this context that children are provided a free public education. Local school boards are delegated responsibility for the daily operations of schools within their districts and are subject to federal and state laws, state board of education policy, as well as federal and state constitutional mandates. The local school board is responsible for formulating policy that enables the district to operate effectively and efficiently in achieving its goals. Federal, state, and local entities have established the context for public education in the United States.

State Board of Education

State boards of education are generally established by the state legislature. Members are normally elected by popular vote and represent respective districts throughout the state. The board is responsible for policy development and general supervision and control of the public schools throughout the state. The board also appoints the chief state school officer.

Chief State School Officer

The chief state school officer is probably the most influential professional educator in the state. Appointed by the state board of education to a set term in most states, he or she is the chief executive officer of the board. His or her primary duty is to execute the educational policies of the state board of education and to oversee the operations of public schools within the state to ensure that they are in compliance with state board policy.

State Department of Education

The state board of education is authorized by the legislature to employ, upon recommendation of the chief state school officer, the professionals necessary to execute the policies of the board to ensure the effective operation of public schools throughout the state. Although there are variations among the states, most state departments consist of divisions of Administration and Finance, Disability Services, Instruction, Legislation and Research, Professional Standards, Audits, and Management among others. The department provides services and support to local school systems in virtually all aspects of local school district operations.

Local Control of Public Schools

Local school boards, created by state statute, are expected to execute state and federal laws and state board policy governing the operations of schools under their jurisdiction. Additionally, they also raise revenue through tax levies and school bonds to construct and maintain facilities, as well as purchase equipment, supplies, and other items essential to the operation of schools. While school board members act as agents of the state, they represent the district electors, parents, citizens, and communities they serve.

School board members are deemed to be state, not local, officers based on the fact that the education function is categorized as one of statewide responsibility. Local school board members are generally elected and hold office by virtue of legislative enactment. The state legislature also prescribes their powers, which may be broadened or limited based on legislative discretion. Local board members may be required to meet certain residency requirements to qualify for election to the board of education.

Local school boards exercise powers, either implied or specified, to manage school districts, including decisions regarding curriculum, although the legal authority for defining the curriculum of public schools resides with the legislature. Based on constitutional provisions in a few states, this duty is shared between the legislature and the state board of education. The legislature may, based on its discretion, prescribe the basic course of study, determine testing standards, and establish graduation requirements. In most cases, state legislatures delegate curriculum matters to state boards of education and, most importantly, with local school districts. Many local school districts in turn have been provided the latitude to establish local school-based management councils that are empowered to make decisions in matters regarding curriculum and instructional practices, textbook selection, and instructional materials.

The local board of education is the legal entity for school districts. The board acts as a corporate body. No single board member has any authority outside of the authority of the board as a whole. The local board of education is a policy-making body that has the responsibility to adopt policies and procedures for the organization and administration of schools within the district. School district policies are generally based on state statute. School leaders have the responsibility to execute these policies. The relationship between the board of education and school leaders is best described as a *legislative-executive relationship.* Since policies provide direction and guidance for teachers, it is imperative that teachers become knowledgeable of policies that impact their professional duties. Teachers are expected to adhere to school and/or district policy. If the legality of a policy is challenged, the burden rests with the school district to defend its policy. However, unawareness of school and district policies does not protect teachers who commit policy violations. In some instances, based on the seriousness of the policy violation, teachers may be disciplined, which may include dismissal for actions that are contrary to board policy.

Teachers as Employees of Local School Boards

School districts are public corporations. Teachers are public employees who are employed by local boards of education. They are agents of the school district in which they are employed. The relationship of teachers to the board of education is contractual. The board of education is the only legal body that has the authority to employ or dismiss school personnel. In some instances, principals recommend teachers for employment positions within their respective schools to the superintendent of schools but these recommendations carry no legal **standing** until the board of education approves the superintendent's recommendation. The superintendent has the prerogative to accept or reject a principal's recommendation so long as the rejection is nondiscriminatory and based on defensible criteria. Employment rejections that are arbitrary or capricious will not receive support by the courts.

School District Rules and Regulations

Boards of education have the implied power to formulate and enforce rules and regulations necessary to facilitate the efficient operation of schools within the district. School board rules and regulations must be reasonable and consistent with state and federal constitutional provisions. It is often difficult to determine the reasonableness of rules. The courts generally presume that the board's actions are reasonable. Since reasonableness is presumed, the burden of proof resides with the party who contests board rules.

The presumption of reasonableness is established in large measure by the courts, based on the view that the role of the courts is not defined as a policy-making one. However, the courts will not hesitate to review school rules and regulations when a substantive challenge arises to determine if they are arbitrary or capricious and in violation of constitutional rights of school personnel and/or students. A reasonable exercise of administrative authority will generally receive support by the courts.

School Board Meetings

School board meetings, as well as minutes of these meetings, are open to the public. Any citizen, including teachers, who desires to do so may attend board meetings. Most states have adopted "sunshine" (or open meeting) laws designed to ensure that the public is informed on matters of public interest. The only exception to open meetings occurs when the board meets in executive session to discuss matters pertaining to personnel issues and other sensitive legal subject matter.

GUIDES

Control of Public Schools

1. The federal government has an interest in public education through the enactment of statutes designed to improve education.
2. Public schools are controlled by the states by virtue of the Tenth Amendment to the U.S. Constitution.
3. The state legislature has complete authority to govern public schools, including but not limited to teacher qualifications, curriculum matters, funding, and student graduation requirements.
4. Each state has police powers, which creates a responsibility for health, safety, and welfare of its citizens.
5. The power to control education is derived from the state's police powers.
6. School boards have specific or implied powers to administer schools within their districts.

7. Local school board members are considered to be state officers because education is a state function.
8. The school board as a policy-making entity has responsibility for guiding the district through development of legally defensible policies and procedures.
9. The local school board is the only entity that has the legal authority to employ or dismiss school personnel.
10. Teachers are public employees based on a contractual relationship with the local school board.
11. Teachers have a leading responsibility to become familiar with and execute school or district policies, rules, and regulations.
12. A violation of policy based on inadequate knowledge is not a justifiable defense for teachers.
13. Teachers may be disciplined, including dismissal for policy violations, based on the seriousness of the violation and its impact on the district.

ENDNOTES

1. *Child Welfare Society of Flint v. Kennedy School Dist.*, 220 Mich. 290, 189 N.W. 1002 (1922).
2. *Leeper v. State*, 103 Tenn. 500, 53 S.W. 962 (1899).
3. *Railroad Co. v. Husen*, 95, U.S. 465, 1877.

two

Instruction and Curriculum Standards

ACADEMIC ISSUES

Curriculum Standards

Minimal curriculum standards in public schools are established by state statute and policy. In almost all cases, certain courses and minimum achievement standards are determined through state statute. Local school districts may establish other standards so long as they do not contradict state requirements. Federal aid programs, such as Title I: Goals 2000 Educate America Act of 1994, Education for Disabled Students, and most recently No Child Left Behind legislation, specify certain standards that must be met to receive federal funds. Also, under the Goals 2000 Educate America Act of 1994, states receive funds if they agree to develop plans to meet certain national goals. Courts are very reluctant to intervene in matters involving public school curricula based on the view that states retain the authority to establish curriculum standards so long as there are no federal constitutional infringements involved.

Virtually every state across the nation has developed academic standards to facilitate student achievement. Increasingly, states have assumed responsibility for identifying the essential knowledge and skills that students must possess to become productive citizens. Supplemental services are provided by a number of states to assist students in meeting their academic needs. In fact, the Elementary and Secondary Education Act of 1965 (ESEA) requires that schools failing to make adequate progress for three consecutive years use a portion of their Title I funds to allow low-income students to enroll in supplemental services. This act is revised every five to seven years. The latest revision passed by Congress in 2001 and signed into law in 2002 is the No Child Left Behind Act aimed at improving the achievement gap between disadvantaged and minority students and their peers, as well as creating greater accountability in education.

NO CHILD LEFT BEHIND ACT OF 2001

On January 8, 2002, President Bush signed into law the No Child Left Behind Act of 2001 (NCLB). This act is considered to be the most sweeping reform since the Elementary and Secondary Education Act was passed in 1965. This new act redefines the federal government's role in K–12 education and again is designed to close the achievement gap between disadvantaged and minority students and their peers. It is based on four basic principles:

1. Stronger accountability for results
2. Increased flexibility and local control
3. Expanded options for parents
4. An emphasis on teaching methods that have been proven to work

Public School Choice

The context for public school choice, supplemental education services, and collective bargaining agreements is the accountability provisions in the Title I program. Under the NCLB Act, each state must establish a definition of "adequate yearly progress" to use each year to determine the achievement of each school district and school. School districts must identify for improvement any Title I school that fails to meet the state's definition of adequate yearly progress for two consecutive years. Such schools, with technical assistance from their school districts, must develop and implement improvement plans incorporating various strategies to strengthen instruction in the core academic subjects in the school and address the specific issues that caused the school to fail. These schools must also provide public school choice and supplemental education services.

In general, in the case of any Title I elementary or secondary school identified for school improvement, the school district is required to provide all students enrolled in the school with the option to transfer to another public school in the school district—which may include a public charter school that has not been identified for improvement. This choice requirement applies unless state law specifically prohibits it based on a key policy letter from the Education Secretary in the U.S. Department of Education in 2002.

Summary and Implications

Accountability

- Each state will implement a statewide accountability system that will be effective in ensuring that all districts and schools make adequate progress. The accountability system includes rewards and sanctions.
- Students cannot be left behind based on:
  a. Race/ethnicity
  b. Disabilities
  c. Limited English proficiency
  d. Economic status (disadvantaged)

Participation

- Students with disabilities who take alternative assessment must participate.
- Schools and districts must average a 95 percent participation rate for all students over a two-year period.

Adequate Yearly Progress

- The same high academic achievement standards will be applied to all students.
- There should be continuous and demonstrated academic improvement for all students.
- Separate measures and annual achievement objectives may be used for all students, including racial/ethnic groups, economically disadvantaged, students with disabilities, and students with limited English proficiency.

Teacher Quality

- All core academic teachers must be highly qualified by 2005–06.
- Core academics include:
  a. English, reading, and languages
  b. Mathematics, science, foreign languages, civics, and government
  c. Economics, arts, history, and geography

Qualified Teachers

The following measures will be used in part to assess qualified teachers:

- A teacher's license
- Success in passing a test
- Content area knowledge:
  a. Academic major or graduate degree in content area
  b. Credits equivalent of academic major (24 hours)
  c. Success in passing test such as Praxis

Paraprofessionals

Paraprofessionals must meet the following requirements:

- Two years of higher education
- Associate's degree
- Test (Parapro through Educational Testing Service)
- High school diploma or its equivalent
- Translators and parent liaisons

Students

Each group of students should meet or exceed annual objectives. Exceptions:

- The number of students who are below proficiency standards should be reduced by 10 percent from the prior year.
- Other indicators may be used to measure progress for subgroups.

Restructuring (Corrective Action)

- If a school fails to make adequate yearly progress after one full year of corrective action, the district must:
  a. Continue to make public school choice available
  b. Continue to make supplemental services available
  c. Prepare a plan to restructure the school

Alternative Governance

- By the beginning of the following school year, the district must implement one of the following alternatives:
  a. Reopen the school as a public charter school
  b. Replace all or most of school staff, including the principal
  c. Enter into a contract with an entity, such as a private management company with a proven record of effectiveness to operate the school
  d. State takeover

VOUCHERS

Although they have increased in use, vouchers have not received support by public school teachers, parents, or the general public, particularly in cases where funds allocated for vouchers compete with public school funding. The theory behind vouchers is that educational funding is channeled to families, which allows them to exercise choices regarding where their children attend school. Vouchers operate under the presumption that parental choice will trigger competition between public and private schools, which will result in improved education for all children. There are concerns among public school officials that vouchers administered by the government tend to create a heavy reliance on the government. With added regulations and the government's intervention into an area that is monitored by the states, vouchers tend to become problematic. It is too early, however, to determine the overall effectiveness of school vouchers. The University of Cleveland's study of vouchers in Indiana found no academic benefit to students after the first year. However, in Milwaukee, both students and parents were far more satisfied with private school education. It may not be surprising to note that students and parents are more satisfied in private schools with selective admission than they are with public schools that admit all students. Selected admission tends to attract the best students, whereas public schools attract all students irrespective of background preparation or readiness.

In a significant ruling, the Supreme Court of Wisconsin held that the expanded Milwaukee voucher program, which allowed 15,000 children to attend any private school, including religious schools, does not violate either state or federal constitutions.[1]

CHARTER SCHOOLS

According to the U.S. Department of Education, charter schools are public schools that emerge through a contract with a state agency or a local school board. The charter establishes the ground rules regarding the operations of the school. The primary advantage of charter schools is autonomy over their operations; they are relieved of rules and regulations that govern public schools. In exchange for flexibility, charter schools are held accountable for achieving outcomes established by the charter, which includes student achievement as a primary goal. The charter school concept is sound. It encourages innovation and creativity without bureaucratic barriers in exchange for measurable and positive student learning outcomes. It is too early to determine if charter schools are effective. In recent years, however, they have experienced a range of problems, including audit findings, failure to follow state guidelines in expending funds, ineffective record-keeping practices, and poor student achievement results, among others.

GUIDES

Instructional Program

1. The state legislature has a responsibility to provide schooling for all children within the state at public expense.
2. The legal authority for defining curriculum resides with the legislature.
3. Courts typically do not intervene in curriculum matters since each state retains the authority to establish curriculum standards. They will intervene only if legitimate constitutional issues emerge.
4. All schools should be held accountable for ensuring that the achievement gap between disadvantaged and minority students is close to that of their peers under the No Child Left Behind Act.
5. Vouchers and charter schools are designed to improve student achievement through providing choice for students and parents.

INTELLECTUAL PROPERTY AND FAIR USE

Intellectual property covers four basic areas: patents, trademarks, designs, and copyright materials. The Copyright Act prohibits unauthorized use of copyrighted material for profit or public display without appropriate payment to or permission from the copyright proprietor. Under the act, the owner of a copyright has the exclusive rights to do and to authorize any of the following:

1. *To reproduce the copyrighted work in copies or phonorecords;*
2. *To prepare derivative works based upon the copyrighted work;*
3. *To distribute copies or phonorecords of the copyrighted work to the public by sale or other transfer of ownership, or by rental, lease, or lending;*
4. *In the case of literary, musical, dramatic, and choreographic works, pantomimes, and motion pictures and other audiovisual works, to perform the copyrighted work publicly; and*

5. *In the case of literary, musical, dramatic, and choreographic works, pantomimes, and pictorial, graphic, or sculptural works, including the individual images of a motion picture or other audiovisual work, to display the copyrighted work publicly.*

The Copyright Act permits educators and libraries to make "fair use" of copyrighted material. Section 107 specifically permits "reproduction in copies or phonorecords . . . for purposes such as . . . teaching (including multiple copies for classroom use), scholarship or research . . .)."[2]

The guidelines are liberal with respect to producing single copies for teaching or research purposes but fairly restrictive regarding the reproduction of multiple copies. For example, reproduction of a poem should not exceed 1,000 words or 10 percent of the work, whichever is less. Additionally, copies should be reproduced by the specific teacher who intends to use the materials for teaching purposes. These guides are not based on law but rather are widely acceptable as meeting the legal intent of the Copyright Act.

The Copyright Act specifies four factors that should be used to determine fair use: (1) the purpose or use relative to whether use is commercial in nature or for nonprofit, educational purposes; (2) the nature of the work; (3) the amount of material extracted from the work in relation to the work as a whole; and (4) the impact of the use on the potential market in relation to the value of the copyrighted work.[3]

Teachers are allowed to produce single copies of copyrighted materials for teaching purposes only. Multiple copies are not permitted. Specialty and extracted materials must be brief in the context of the type of work involved and should be initiated by the teacher who intends to use the materials. Additionally, the use of the materials must be applied in a manner that makes it unreasonable to seek permission by the authors to use the materials. Copies should be restricted to one course. Care must be exercised by the teacher to avoid extracting all materials from a single author. Duplicating materials should not be produced to avoid purchasing a book or any other consumable work.

Copying Computer Software

Copyright laws also affect computer software. Teachers should not reproduce copies of software for students from an original program to serve as a backup copy. This is prohibited under the Copyright Act. Most school districts have purchased site licenses to provide protection for the use of software. This type of license is essentially a contractual agreement with a software company where a fee is negotiated for the use of educational software. Under the contractual agreement, a reasonable number of copies may be reproduced for educational purposes.

USE OF THE INTERNET FOR INSTRUCTION

An important component of the instructional program involves the use of electronic technology. Information technology has drastically altered teaching and learning, as well as the school's administrative processes. It has changed the fabric of school operations. Internet access has increased dramatically in public schools throughout the nation. Given the widespread use and application of the Internet and the potential for abuse, students and parents should be required to review and agree on rules governing access and use of the Internet.

School or District Responsibility

Schools or school districts should develop and enforce an acceptable use policy. This policy should govern all electronic programming such as e-mail and general access to the Internet by students and employees. The board of education will generally not incur liability if it has filtering software installed that may inadvertently fail. However, measures must be taken to correct the failure. By standard practice, each district or school should establish a process for modifying the filtering system or defiltering Internet access for students when it is educationally appropriate.

At a minimum, the filtering system should restrict access to Internet sites or chatrooms that contain

- Offensive messages
- Obscene language
- Sexual acts
- Violence
- Sexual attire
- Crime
- Nudity
- Intolerance
- Harassing messages

Teacher's Responsibility

Teachers have a responsibility to select material that is appropriate based on the age and maturity of the students and consistent with course objectives. Consequently, teachers must preview material and sites that students are required to access to determine the appropriateness of material contained within the site. Teachers should also provide guidance by identifying and listing resources to assist students in their learning activities. They should monitor content that students access on the Internet and follow approved procedures when student violations occur.

Parents' Responsibility

Parents should be aware of guidelines and instructions for student protection while using the Internet. Although the board's or school's acceptable use policy will restrict access to inappropriate material, there is a wide range of material available to students on the Internet. Parents must assume a leadership role in instilling proper values to their children and instructing their children regarding materials that are acceptable and those that are not. Parents should also monitor Internet use at home to ensure that their children are following the parents' directives. Home monitoring by parents will reinforce acceptable use policies implemented by school personnel. Cooperation and coordination of Internet use between parents and teachers will generally yield more favorable results regarding Internet use by students.

GUIDES

Use of the Internet for Instruction

1. The fair use concept provides a degree of flexibility for teachers to use certain materials without infringement for teaching purposes.
2. School officials should be certain that the Internet use policy is clearly written and communicated to parents and students.
3. Parents, teachers, and students, where appropriate, should be involved in drafting Internet use policies.
4. Policies should inform teachers, students, and parents of their responsibilities regarding enforcement of Internet use policies.
5. Due process and fundamental fairness should be observed in enforcing Internet use policies involving students.
6. Specific disciplinary measures for inappropriate use of the Internet should be spelled out in the district's acceptable use policy.

7. Students should be cautioned that personal contact information regarding themselves or others should not be posted on the Internet without prior written consent from the parent or legal guardian.
8. Students should be informed that they should promptly disclose to their teachers any inappropriate messages they receive on the Internet.
9. Users should be informed by policy that the following activities are prohibited:
    a. Subverting network security
    b. Bypassing restrictions established by school officials
    c. Using the Internet for illegal purposes such as drug transactions, obtaining alcohol for minors, and gang-related activities
    d. Seeking information about passwords of others
    e. Using obscene, vulgar, rude, threatening, or abusive language
    f. Taking writings of others and presenting them without prior written permission (plagiarizing)
    g. Using the Internet to promote personal or commercial enterprises

GRADING AND ACADEMIC REQUIREMENTS

Courts traditionally have been reluctant to interfere in cases involving academic matters. The prevailing view held by the courts is that professional educators are better prepared to make decisions regarding academic issues, particularly those involving student evaluation. Requirements regarding progress from one grade to another typically are not reviewable by the courts unless there is substantial evidence of unreasonableness. For example, the Fourth Circuit Court of Appeals refused to intervene in the failure of a school district to promote to the third grade those students who failed to pass a reading-level test.[4] The court respected the educational judgment of professional educators, even though the students' intelligence indicated that they were capable of reading at the third-grade level. They could not be promoted until they demonstrated mastery of the requisite reading skill. One court observed that academic matters, by their very nature, are more subjective and evaluative than typical issues presented in disciplinary decisions, and such academic judgments should be left to professional educators.[5]

Student Testing

It is well established that the state has the authority to promulgate promotion and graduation requirements. Oftentimes, standardized tests are used to determine student competencies. If the measures are reasonable and nondiscriminatory, they will generally be supported by the courts. Educators are provided considerable discretion in matters relating to appropriate academic requirements. By and large, courts do not feel equipped to evaluate academic performance issues.[6] Therefore, courts limit themselves to addressing issues relating to due process, discriminatory impact, and arbitrary or capricious acts by school personnel. Thus, the state's authority to develop and assess student performance standards is not debatable.

Grade Reduction for Absences

Excessive absenteeism by students poses a challenge for school officials who oftentimes resort to grade reductions as a means to limit excessive absences. Courts will generally support reasonable policies regarding grade reduction for excessive absences if they do not conflict with state statute. School district policy should provide guidance for teachers in cases involving grade reductions for student absenteeism.

Grade Reduction for Unexcused Absences

School rules that penalize students academically for unexcused absences, or truancy, are not uncommon. Courts have been more supportive of schools on this type of rule rather than one that mandates grade reduction based on general misconduct. In fact, courts have been quite consistent since the mid-1970s in ruling against school districts for grade reduction related to misconduct. Thus, school districts must be certain that their rules in this area are carefully drawn. The following cases illustrate this point.

In a New Jersey school district, school board policy mandated that a student receive a zero in all subjects on those days he or she is truant from school. The student can make up any tests he or she may have missed on such days, but the zero had to be used when grades were averaged for the term. In ruling for the student who challenged the rule, the New Jersey Commissioner of Education found the penalty to be excessive.[7] In some instances a student could receive a failing grade in a class for even a single absence. A major reason the school board lost its case appears to be related to the severity of the penalty rather than the use of grade reduction in general.

Grade Reduction for Academic Misconduct

A number of school districts formulated policies requiring grade reductions for misconduct. An example of the courts' position regarding grade reduction was illustrated in the following case.[8] Two students participated as guitar players in the high school band program. The band director prohibited band members from departing from the planned musical program during band performances, and specifically forbade guitar solos during the performances. In direct defiance of those rules, the two students played two unauthorized guitar pieces at a band program. The discipline they received for this infraction caused them both to receive an F for the band course, and that F prevented one student from graduating with honors. Both students appealed the district court's decision, which favored the school. The court concluded that the school's actions violated no right under the federal civil rights statutes.

A different case arose in Indiana in which a student's grade was reduced as punishment for alcohol-related misconduct. The student's parents brought suit against the district and moved for summary judgment. The district court held that a high school rule mandating a 4 percent reduction in grades for each day a student had been suspended for alcohol use during school hours was invalid and a violation of substantive due process. The court stated further that the policy was arbitrary and that the school failed to demonstrate a reasonable relationship between the use of alcohol during school hours and a reduction in grades.[9] In an earlier case, the New Jersey Commissioner ruled that the use of grades as punishment is usually ineffective in producing the desired results and is educationally indefensible. Whatever system of grades a school may devise will have serious limitations at best, and it must not be further limited by attempting to serve disciplinary purposes also.[10]

Physical Punishment for Poor Academic Performance

Physical punishment of public school students for failure to maintain acceptable academic standards has not received support by the courts. Courts have consistently ruled against teachers and school officials for the use of physical punishment when the student's behavior did not involve improper conduct. For example, one court ruled against physical punishment of a student who failed to perform at an athletically desired level, even though the coach considered the punishment to be instructive and a source of encouragement to the student.[11] U.S. courts have consistently held that public school students should not be physically punished for conduct not related to disciplinary infractions. Furthermore, students should not be physically punished for failure to complete homework or other assignments. School officials may adopt policies calling for academic penalties such as a loss of credit for failure to meet academic assignments but under no circumstances should physical punishment be inflicted in cases involving academic matters.

GUIDES

Grading and Academic Requirements

1. Competency tests are supported by the courts where there is no evidence of discriminatory intent.
2. Assignment of academic grades as a punitive measure for misbehavior is illegal and indefensible.
3. Students may be penalized academically for unexcused absences or truancy if state statute permits. However, policies in this area should be carefully drawn to ensure fairness.
4. Physical punishment for poor performance has not been supported by the courts. Physical punishment, when used, must be associated with improper conduct.

EDUCATIONAL MALPRACTICE

Over the last three decades, educational malpractice has emerged as a formidable threat to educators. Increasingly, parents have brought suits on behalf of their children, alleging that teachers were either negligent or incapable of providing competent instruction, proper placement, and classification of their children. In these cases, students have charged that they suffered academic injury by being denied the full benefits of a proper education.

Although numerous suits have been filed in the past, to date no case has been won by parents or students. However, with the emergence of school-based management, national teaching standards, No Child Left Behind, greater teacher accountability, and emphasis on professionalism in education, the prospect of a successful malpractice challenge may be greatly heightened.

Educational malpractice generally is considered to be any unprofessional conduct or lack of sufficient skill in the performance of professional duties. It represents a different type of injury to students. This type of injury is not physical but emotional, psychological, or educational, resulting from poor teaching, improper placement, or inappropriate testing procedures.

Since the courts have prescribed duties for teachers to *instruct, supervise*, and *provide for the safety of children*, a breach of these duties resulting in injury to students may form adequate grounds for a liability suit. Teacher liability, however, may differ from state to state.

In cases involving alleged academic injury to students, courts have faced the very difficult task of determining exactly where actual fault lies. Does the alleged injury rest with the student's inability to acquire basic or minimal skills due to his or her lack of ability or motivation? Or does the alleged injury rest with the teacher's inability to meet minimal standards of teaching? Further, if teachers are determined to be at fault, is it a single teacher, a select few, or all teachers involved in a child's educational experiences who are to be blamed? Because of these difficulties, courts have failed to support charges of malpractice. Also, because teachers historically have had no direct influence over school policies, curriculum, working conditions, or resource acquisition, they could not reasonably be held to a strict standard of liability. However, with the emergence of teacher empowerment, school-based management, and national teaching and certification standards, the courts may be better able to determine if liability has occurred and precisely where it occurred. Teachers should be certain that skills are taught and retaught in instances where students fail to master the required skills. Teachers should also document that these skills were taught. Remediation and documentation are important components of the teaching and learning process.

GUIDES

Educational Malpractice

1. School districts should develop quality standards of practice as a means to guide the instructional program within schools.
2. Teachers should be certain that they are well prepared and highly focused on their instructional duties.

3. Teachers should ensure that all required competencies and skills are taught in the classroom.

4. Systemwide remediation should be provided for students who fail to master required skills and competencies or for those who have difficulty learning.

5. School districts should make informed decisions regarding the appropriateness of curriculum, textbooks, and instructional policies.

6. Teachers should develop flexible and varied instructional strategies and techniques to meet individual needs of students.

7. Districts should use well-prepared promotion and retention standards as guides to decisions affecting student progress.

8. Teachers should be certain that curricula objectives are translated into topics actually taught in the classroom.

9. School districts should avoid inappropriate testing procedures that could result in misclassification or inappropriate placement of students.

10. Proper means should be developed to monitor instructional practices to improve the overall educational delivery system.

ENDNOTES

1. *Warner Jackson et al. v. Superintendent of Public Instruction*, 213 Wis. 2d 1, 570 N.W. 2d 407 (1998).
2. 17 U.S.C. § 101 et seq. (1996).
3. Ibid.
4. *Sandlin v. Johnson*, 643 F. 2d 1027 (4th Cir. 1981).
5. *Board of Curators of the University of Missouri v. Horowitz*, 435 U.S. 78, 985, S.Ct. 948 (1978).
6. Ibid.
7. *Minorities v. Board of Education of Phillipsburg*, N.J. Commissioner of Ed. (1972).
8. *Dunn and McCollough v. Fairfield Community High School District No. 225*, 158 F. 3d 962 (U.S. App. 1998).
9. *Smith v. School City of Hobart et al. Defendants*, 811 F. Supp. 391, 80 Ed. Law Rept. 839 (Ind. 1993).
10. *Wermuth v. Bernstein and Board of Education of the Township of Livingston* (Dec. N.J. Comm. Ed., 1965).
11. *Hogenson v. Williams*, 542 S.W. 2d 256 (Tex. App. 1976).

three

Religion and Public Schools

PRAYER, BIBLE READING, AND RELIGIOUS SYMBOLS

The tension between church and state issues relates to the requirement that the government maintain a neutral position toward religion. In 1879, the Supreme Court in the landmark *Reynolds v. United States* invoked Jefferson's view that there be a wall of separation between church and state.[1]

The First Amendment serves as the basis for delineating certain individual religious rights and freedoms, as well as governmental prohibitions regarding religion. The First Amendment to the United States Constitution states, "Congress shall make no laws respecting an establishment of religion or prohibiting the free exercise thereof; or abridging the freedom of speech, or of the press; or the right of the people peaceably to assemble and to petition the government for a redress of grievances."

Although the initial intent of the First Amendment prohibited Congress from making laws supporting religion or prohibiting the rights of individuals to exercise their religious rights, the United States Supreme Court, in a compelling 1940 decision, *Cantwell v. Connecticut,* held that this prohibition aimed at Congress also applied to the States as well.[2] The Fourteenth Amendment made the First Amendment applicable to state action, thus providing the same constitutional guarantees to citizens against state infringement of their religious rights by prohibiting the establishment of religious practices in public schools.

The First Amendment contains two essential clauses regarding religion: the establishment clause and the free exercise clause. The *establishment clause* prohibits the state from passing laws that aid a religion or show preference of one religion over another; the *free exercise clause* prohibits the state from interfering with individual religious freedoms.

The combined effect of these two clauses compels public schools, as state agencies, to maintain a neutral position regarding religious matters in their daily operations. This means that the state can neither aid nor inhibit religion—it must adhere to the principle of neutrality. Since the *Cantwell* decision, which held that the Fourteenth Amendment makes the First Amendment applicable to state action, the establishment clause has significant implications for the administration of public schools.

The establishment clause essentially raises concerns in instances where school personnel act as state agents. When school personnel are not acting in this capacity, the establishment clause does not restrict their individual religious freedom. Freedom of speech, association, and religion protects school personnel, just as it protects the religious activities of other citizens.

School-Sponsored Prayer

The issue of prayer in public schools was addressed in a landmark case in the early 1960s by the United States Supreme Court. Prior to this time, prayer was routinely offered in public schools across the nation and generally supported by the courts. In spite of the eventful *Engel* decision, the inclusion of school prayer continues to be challenged by Congress, state legislatures, and citizens as they persist in seeking creative ways to support prayer in public schools.[3] The United States Supreme Court first addressed prayer in public schools in the famous *Engel v. Vitale* case. In 1962, the New York Board of Regents required the reading of a school-sponsored, nondenominational, voluntary prayer that was to be recited by each class in the presence of the classroom teacher. This prayer was composed by the State Board of Regents and read as follows:

> *Almighty God, we acknowledge our dependence upon thee and we beg thy blessings upon us, our parents, our teachers and our country.*

Those students who did not wish to recite the prayer were excused from participation. This practice was challenged by parents on the grounds that it violated the establishment clause of the First Amendment and was in conflict with the beliefs and religious orientation of some students. The U.S. Supreme Court held for the parents in ruling that the prayer was religious in nature and did in fact violate the establishment clause of the First Amendment.

The Court held that the state's support of prayer recitation in the public schools was illegal. Although this ruling has been consistently reinforced by numerous court decisions since 1962, it remains a highly contested issue as persistent lawmakers in many states continue their efforts to reinstate some form of prayer in public schools.

Consequently, school prayer remains at the center of controversy in public schools. The courts have been consistent in holding that prayer that is sanctioned by public schools is a violation of the establishment clause of the First Amendment. Therefore, school personnel must remain neutral in matters involving prayer in public schools. However, the courts have been somewhat consistent in holding that private devotional activities initiated by students with no involvement or encouragement by school personnel that do not disrupt school activities are permissible. Whether prayer in public school is permissible largely depends on who schedules it. Students may do so under the free exercise clause without school involvement, whereas school personnel may not, without violating the establishment clause of the First Amendment.

Silent Prayer and Meditation

In recent years, attempts also have been made by state legislatures to support some form of state-sponsored voluntary prayer or meditation in public schools. Their efforts, however, have been largely unsuccessful. Numerous challenges to these types of statutes or practices have been led by opposing parents and citizens. Their challenges cover a full range of school activities, such as meditation and prayer at school-sponsored athletic events and graduation ceremonies, both of which will be discussed later in this chapter.

The United States Supreme Court, in 1985, responded to silent meditation and prayer by ruling in the *Wallace v. Jaffree* case that a period of silence set aside for meditation or voluntary prayer in the public school is a violation of the First Amendment.[4] Based on the U.S. Supreme Court's ruling in the *Jaffree* case, teachers must therefore refrain from endorsing any school-sanctioned silent prayer and meditation activities.

Prayer at School Events

In the 1960s and 1970s, courts were less inclined to rule against the use of prayer at baccalaureate and graduation services. These activities were viewed as traditional and ceremonial and in many cases consistent with community sentiments. However, in the mid-1980s, lower courts began to rule against prayer at these activities, holding that the use of prayer violated the establishment clause. In a leading Rhode Island 1992 case, *Lee v. Weisman*,[5] the Supreme Court invalidated the school district's policy that allowed clergy to be invited to deliver invocations and benedictions at middle and high school graduation ceremonies. The clergy's participation was held to be a violation of the establishment clause. The Court further noted that, in some instances, students were required to attend these ceremonies with possible peer pressure influencing them to participate. The Court was not convinced that voluntary attendance lessened the impact of the constitutional violation.

The Supreme Court's ban on prayer at graduation ceremonies led school officials to seek more creative methods to include prayer in these ceremonies. For example, in a significant development, the U.S. Supreme Court let stand a stunning appeals court decision permitting student-initiated, student-led prayer at the Clear Creek Independent School District's graduation ceremonies in Texas. In this decision, *Jones v. Clear Creek* in 1992, a federal appeals court ruled that a Texas school district's policy of allowing each high school senior class to decide whether to offer student-initiated and student-led prayers at its graduation ceremony does not violate the First Amendment ban on the government's establishment of religion. The factors that influenced the Court's ruling were as follows:

1. The prayer was strictly initiated by students.
2. School personnel played no role and were not involved in any aspects of the decision to offer prayer.
3. The school had no policy calling for student-initiated prayer at graduation ceremonies but rather an opportunity for students to make a two-minute speech at the beginning and end of the ceremony.
4. The student's speech was not censored.
5. Students possess First Amendment rights to free expression.

In a contrasting case, the U.S. Supreme Court in 2000 invalidated student-led prayer at graduation and other school events in the *Santa Fe v. Jane Doe* case.[6] In this case, there was evidence that the school supported, by school policy, the delivery of prayer over the public address system by the Student Council Chaplain at each home game. The Fifth Circuit held that the policy was invalid because it violated the establishment clause of the First Amendment.

In conclusion, the courts have permitted student-initiated prayer involving no school personnel in *Jones v. Clear Creek*[7] in Texas as well as a two-minute opening and closing remark by graduating classes delivered by student volunteers in *Adler v. Duval County School Board*[8] in Florida in 1994. By allowing each high school senior class to decide whether to offer a student-initiated and student-led prayer at its graduation, in these cases, does not violate the First Amendment ban on the government's establishment of religion. The facts revealed that the district's policy had a secular purpose of safeguarding the free speech rights of participating students. The courts will usually rely on criteria derived in the 1971 landmark *Lemon v. Kurtzman* case even though it involved aid to parochial schools. This test is often relied on by courts to determine the legality of a practice involving religion in public schools. Based on the *Lemon* standards, it was determined that a law, policy, or practice must meet the following criteria to be legally valid regarding religion:

1. *It must have a secular purpose.*
2. *It must neither advance nor prohibit/inhibit religion.*
3. *It must not create excessive entanglement.*[9]

Educators no longer enjoy the freedom they once possessed in planning school programs based solely on community values and standards. The courts in recent years have abandoned community sentiment in favor of constitutionality. The Supreme Court's position in *Jones v. Clear Creek* and *Adler v. Duval*, however, may provide an opportunity for some communities to decide if they wish to have students assume the decision-making role. For now, at least, under certain conditions, voluntary student-led prayer at graduation ceremonies may be permissible. This is a major victory for proponents of prayer and perhaps an end to some of the controversy involving prayer at graduation ceremonies.

School-Sponsored Bible Reading

In 1963, the U.S. Supreme Court addressed the constitutionality of the practice of Bible reading in public schools. Two similar cases reached the Supreme Court during the same period of time. The *Abington School District v. Schempp* in 1965 involved a challenge regarding the validity of a Pennsylvania state statute that required the reading of 10 verses of the Bible without comment at the opening of each school day. A companion case, *Murray v. Curlett,* challenged the actual practice of daily Bible reading in the schools of Maryland.[10]

The Supreme Court invoked the *primary effect* test to determine the impact of the statute and practice relating to each case. The primary effect test raises the question of whether the primary purpose of a law or practice has the effect of advancing or inhibiting religion and creating excessive entanglement between church and state. If the response to these questions is affirmative, the principle of neutrality has been breached and the act is considered to be an impermissible establishment of religion and a violation of the First Amendment. The court did, however, indicate in the *Schempp* case that the use of the Bible as a *historical, literary, ethics, or philosophical document* is permissible if a secular purpose is clearly served. Therefore, teachers may use the Bible as a teaching tool if used as a literary document or a historical document. So long as the Bible serves a secular purpose and is related to the subject taught by a teacher, its use is permissible.

Religious Symbols

Public schools may not display religious exhibits such as paintings, statutes, pictures, or other visual materials. It may be appropriate, however, for public school teachers to acknowledge and explain the various holidays of all cultural and religious groups as a unit in cultural heritage or some other related subject, so long as a secular purpose is served.

Public school teachers should refrain from the use of religious symbols or pictures, even in conjunction with discussing the various holidays. A case could be made that the presence of the crucifix creates a religious atmosphere in the classroom. The presence of any type of religious symbol or picture would violate the principle of neutrality. Pictures of religious events may also create a devotional atmosphere.

Religious Displays

Religious displays are prohibited in public school settings. To illustrate, a Michigan secondary school displayed a picture of Jesus Christ in a hallway near the gymnasium. This picture had been in place for more than 30 years. A student filed a lawsuit seeking an order to have it removed, based on a violation of the establishment clause to the First Amendment.

The court held for the student by ordering that the picture be removed. The school appealed to the U.S. Court of Appeals for the Sixth Circuit.

The school argued that the plaintiff had graduated and the issue was moot. The court disagreed, finding that the student did, on occasion, visit the school for various sports events and other school activities. Further, the picture had the potential to offend others. The court in its ruling relied on the three-pronged test found in the *Lemon* case. In finding that the display served no secular purpose, it served to advance religion and created excessive entanglement—all violations of the First Amendment. The order was affirmed.[11]

With respect to displays, it would be permissible, however, to employ seasonal decorations such as reindeer, snow, pine trees, wreaths, eggs, or bunny rabbits. These are considered merely reflections of the joy and merriment associated with various holidays so long as they are not used to meet a religious purpose.

Public schools may not erect any type of religious display on school property, such as the Nativity scene or the crucifix. However, in 1963, one such display was held by a district in New York to be a mere passive accommodation of religion.[12] This court supported the erection of a Nativity scene on school grounds. The posture of the courts today would not support such a finding. It is indisputable that the presence of a Nativity scene on school property violates the separation of church and state by demonstrating preference of one religion over another and a clear violation of the establishment clause of the First Amendment.

Ten Commandments

Two early court decisions, one at the federal district level and the other by the U.S. Supreme Court, held that posting of the Ten Commandments in a public school is unconstitutional. North Dakota passed a law requiring the display of a placard that contained the Ten Commandments of the Christian and Jewish religions. The statute called for this display to be located in a conspicuous place in every classroom in public schools. The district court ruled that this practice violated the establishment clause of the First Amendment.[13] Interestingly, the State Supreme Court of Kentucky in *Stone v. Graham*[14] in 1980 reached a tie decision regarding a statute that required posting the Ten Commandments in public school classrooms. The tie proved to be insignificant when the U.S. Supreme Court in a 5–4 decision held that this practice was unconstitutional and a violation of the establishment clause of the First Amendment.

Prayer at School Board Meetings

School boards that open their meetings with prayer are violating the Constitution's First Amendment establishment clause. The Sixth Circuit Court of Appeals relied on a series of prayer cases in rendering its decision. A school board initiated a practice of inviting clergy to offer prayer at its meetings, which was challenged by a student and a teacher who frequently attended board meetings. The Federal District Court upheld the board's practice, finding that the meetings resembled legislative sessions rather than school events and relying on the 1983 U.S. Supreme Court ruling that allowed official prayers at the beginning of state legislative sessions. The student and teacher appealed to the Sixth Circuit, which ruled that board meetings were held on school property, were regularly attended by students, and did not resemble legislative sessions. The court further emphasized that board meetings had a function that was uniquely directed toward students and school matters making it necessary for students to attend such meetings on many occasions. The Sixth Circuit Court stated that prayer at school board meetings was potentially coercive to students in attendance. The Circuit Court reversed the District Court's ruling, holding that prayer has the tendency to endorse Christianity while excessively entangling the board in religious matters.[15] Consequently, this practice was held to be unconstitutional.

GUIDES

Prayer and Bible Use in School

1. Legally defensible guidelines should be developed based on the U.S. Supreme Court decision addressing student-initiated prayer at athletic contests and other school events.
2. School personnel should not rely on customs and community expectations in encouraging student-initiated prayer at school events.
3. Voluntary student-initiated prayer is permissible at school events when not endorsed by school personnel.
4. School officials should respond judiciously if alerted that school personnel are encouraging students to offer voluntary prayer at school-sponsored events.

5. Prayer at school board meetings violates the establishment clause, creates excessive entanglement, and cannot be justified on the basis that such meetings are similar to legislative sessions rather than school events.

6. Teachers may use the Bible for secular purposes in conjunction with a history, literature, or related class. The use of the Bible as a religious document violates the establishment clause of the First Amendment.

RELIGIOUS ACTIVITIES AND HOLIDAY PROGRAMS

The observance of holidays by public schools is clearly an unconstitutional activity if conducted in a devotional atmosphere. The First Amendment prohibits states from either aiding religion or showing preference of one religion over another. Public schools may not celebrate religious holidays. There should be no worship or devotional services, religious pageants or plays of any nature held in the school. However, certain programs may be conducted if a secular purpose is clearly served.

For example, the district court upheld the school's Christmas program in South Dakota when certain parents challenged the religious content of a Christmas program that was sponsored, based on school district policy. The district's policy was challenged on the grounds that it violated the establishment clause of the First Amendment. The U.S. District Court of South Dakota held for the school district in ruling that the performance of music containing religious content does not within itself constitute a religious activity, so long as it served an educational rather than a religious purpose.[16]

Schools, however, are prohibited from the use of sacred music that occurs in a devotional setting. This type of music may be sung or played as a part of a music appreciation class, however, so long as a secular purpose is served. School choirs and assemblies may be permitted to sing or play holiday carols if these activities are held for entertainment purposes rather than religious purposes.

Distribution of Religious Materials

Public school personnel are not permitted to distribute religious materials, such as pamphlets or religious literature, on school premises. Such practice is a clear violation of the establishment clause. Public school officials also may not allow religious groups to distribute religious materials on school grounds. Support of such practices would suggest that the school embraces religion and could suggest preference of one religion over another. Again, the principle of neutrality commands that schools assume a neutral position, neither supporting religion nor prohibiting individual students from exercising their religious rights. Two cases illustrate the courts' posture regarding the distribution of religious materials.

One case involving the distribution of religious material arose in Florida when an elementary student brought religious pamphlets to distribute to her classmates. When the elementary student requested, through her teacher, to be allowed to distribute the pamphlets, they were confiscated and carried to the principal, who subsequently destroyed them, indicating that he could not permit the distribution of religious material at school.

The student and her mother filed a suit in the U.S. District Court seeking a preliminary injunction against enforcement of the policy. The court held that the motion was premature and that the policy had never been applied by the school. The Eleventh Circuit Court affirmed the district court's decision. The district court then addressed the student's request for a permanent injunction against enforcing the policy. The court discerned that the policy was a content-based prior restraint ban on free speech that could be justified only with a showing that the literature would materially or substantially disrupt the operations of the school or infringe on the rights of other students.

In the absence of this showing, the school district's policy, as expected, could not be supported under the law. The First Amendment to the U.S. Constitution prohibits the government from inhibiting the free exercise of religion. There was no evidence that the distribution of the religious pamphlets interfered *materially* or *substantially* with school operations. The court held for the student by issuing a permanent injunction against the enforcement of the policy and also awarded nominal damages and attorney fees.[17]

The other leading case, *Tudor v. Board of Education*[18] in 1954, arose in New Jersey where the highest court in New Jersey struck down an attempt by Gideons International to distribute the Gideon Bible throughout the public schools.

Pledge of Allegiance

A 2002 landmark case, *Newdow v. United States,* challenging the daily ritual of reciting the Pledge of Allegiance emerged in the Ninth Circuit Court in California regarding the constitutionality of the inclusion of *under God*. The outcome of the ruling in this case had a profound affect on public schools, state and federal governments, as well as American citizens in general. Forty-nine states filed briefs supporting the Pledge of Allegiance.

This case arose when Michael R. Newdow, an atheist and a noncustodial parent, filed a suit on behalf of his 8-year-old daughter challenging the inclusion of the words *under God* in the pledge. A panel of the U.S. Court of Appeals for the Ninth Circuit in San Francisco created quite a controversy when it ruled 2–1 that the inclusion of *under God* was an unconstitutional establishment of religion by the government.

The defendants were the Elk Grove Unified School District, the State of California, the U.S. Congress, and President George W. Bush. The 8-year-old girl's mother, Sandra Banning, publicly confirmed that her daughter had no religious objection to reciting the pledge in school. Newdow and Banning, the child's parents, were never married. Both held informal custody of their daughter until February 2003, after which time sole custody was awarded to Ms. Banning. A California Superior Court barred Newdow from naming his daughter as defendant.

The Bush Administration defended the words *under God* in the Pledge of Allegiance and asked the Supreme Court to uphold the daily recitation of the pledge. The administration's rationale was that reciting the Pledge of Allegiance is a patriotic exercise and not a religious testimonial. In addition, the administration said that the reference to "one nation under God" in the Pledge of Allegiance is an official acknowledgment of what all students may properly be taught in school regardless of their religious affiliation. The American Center for Law filed court papers on behalf of members of Congress. The Ninth Circuit Court of Appeals delayed implementing its decision until the Supreme Court ruled on the case.[19]

On June 14, 2004, the U.S. Supreme Court overturned the Ninth Circuit Court's decision on technical grounds and preserved the contested phrase *one nation under God* in the Pledge of Allegiance. The Supreme Court ruled that Newdow, the plaintiff, had no legal standing to challenge the pledge, since he was not the custodial parent of his then 10-year-old daughter and could not legally represent her. This ruling failed to address whether the inclusion of the reference to God was an impermissible practice involving an unconstitutional blending of church and state. Consequently, the U.S. Supreme Court's ruling does not prevent a future lawsuit challenging the inclusion of the phrase *one nation under God* in the pledge. In fact, another challenge has emerged by Newdow and others who oppose the pledge of allegiance. At least for now, millions of school children who desire to do so may continue to recite the Pledge of Allegiance in public schools since the U.S. Supreme Court decision in *West Virginia State Board of Education v. Barnette* case in 1943 held that public school officials may not require students to salute and pledge allegiance to the flag.[20] These activities must be strictly voluntary.

GUIDES

Religious Activities

1. School-sponsored holiday programs are permitted if they do not create a religious atmosphere and if they have a secular purpose.
2. School districts may find it difficult to justify the posting of the Ten Commandments or other references to God as meeting a purely secular purpose.
3. Religious pageants, displays, or symbols will not meet the constitutional requirements of neutrality by school officials. However, statues or pictures may be used to teach art form if taught as a secular activity.
4. The distribution of religious material by external groups is illegal if the distribution occurs on school premises. However, a student may be allowed to distribute religious pamphlets if the distribution does not interfere with normal school activities or create material or substantial disruption.
5. School officials must respect the free exercise rights of students, unless the exercise of those rights violates the rights of others or disrupts the educational process.
6. Educators must refrain from any activity that would create an unclear line of separation between school activities and religious activities.
7. Students may not be compelled to recite the Pledge of Allegiance based on their right to freedom of expression.

ENDNOTES

1. *Reynolds v. United States,* 98 U.S. (8 OTTO) 145 (1879).
2. *Cantwell v. Connecticut,* 310 U.S. 296 (1940).
3. *Engel v. Vitale,* 370 U.S. 421, 82 S.Ct. 1261 (1962).
4. *Wallace v. Jaffree,* 472 U.S. 38, 105 S.Ct. 2479 (1985).
5. *Lee v. Weisman,* 505 U.S. 577 (1992).

6. *Santa Fe Independent School District v. Jane Doe,* 120 S.Ct. 2266; 147 L.Ed. 2d 295 (2000).

7. *Jones v. Clear Creek Independent School District,* 977 F.2d 963 (5th Cir. 1992).

8. *Adler v. Duval County School Board,* 851 F.Supp. 446 (M.D. Fla. 1994).

9. *Lemon v. Kurtzman and Early v. Dicenso,* 403, U.S. 602, 91 S.Ct. 2105 (1971).

10. *School District of Abington Township v. Schempp; Murray v. Curlett,* 374 U.S. 203, 83 S.Ct. 1650 (1965).

11. *Washegisic v. Bloomingdale Public Schools* 33f. 3d 679 (6th Cir. 1994).

12. *Lawrence v. Buchmuller,* 40 Misc. 2d 300, 243 N.Y.S. 2d 87, 91 (Sup. Ct. 1963).

13. *Ring v. Grand Forks School District No. 1,* 483 F.Supp. 272 (N.D. 1980).

14. *Stone v. Graham,* 599 S.W. 2d. 157 (Ky 1980).

15. *Coles v. Cleveland Board of Education,* 1999, WL 144262 (6th Cir. 1999).

16. *Florey v. Sioux Falls School District,* 464 F.Supp. 911 (D.S.D. 1979).

17. *Johnson-Loehner v. O'Brien,* 859 F.Supp. 575 (M.D. Fla. 1994).

18. *Tudor v. Board of Education of Borough of Rutherford* 14 N.J. 31,100 A.2d 857 (1953). Cert. den. 348 U.S. 816, 75 S.Ct. 25, 99 L. Ed. 664 (1954).

19. *Newdow v. United States,* 315 F. 3d 497 (C.A. 9, 2002).

20. *West Virginia State Board of Education v. Barnette,* 319 U.S. 624, 63 S.Ct. 1178 (1943).

CHAPTER

four

Students, the Law, and Public Schools

School officials are granted broad powers to establish rules and regulations governing student conduct in public schools. These powers, however, are not absolute. They are subject to the standard of *reasonableness.* Generally, rules are deemed to be reasonable if they are necessary to maintain an orderly and peaceful school environment and advance the educational process. The courts, in determining the enforceability of policies, rules, and regulations, require evidence of *sufficient justification* by school officials of the need to enforce the policy, rule, or regulation. Since students enjoy many of the same constitutional rights as adults, courts have been very diligent in ensuring that students' constitutional rights be protected.

Although school rules are necessary to ensure proper order and decorum, they should not be so broad and nebulous as to allow for *arbitrary and inconsistent interpretation.* Fundamental fairness requires that students know what behavior is required of them by school personnel. Rules should be sufficiently definite in providing students with adequate information regarding expected behavior.

Further, in determining whether policies or regulations are fair and reasonable, it is necessary to assess them in the context of their application. Whether a rule or regulation is legally defensible depends on the fact situation.

The concept of *in loco parentis* (in place of parent) has permitted educators to promulgate rules that allow them to exercise a reasonable degree of control over students under their supervision. This concept, however, is not without limits. School officials and teachers do not fully occupy the place of the parent. *Their control or jurisdiction is limited to school functions and activities.* Although *in loco parentis* is considered a viable concept, it does require prudence on the part of school officials and teachers. Prudence in this instance implies that educators' actions must be consistent with those of the average parent under the same or similar circumstances. Children are subject to reasonable rules and regulations promulgated by school officials, but they do enjoy personal rights that must be recognized and respected. However, *in loco parentis* does allow teachers to control student conduct in the classroom so long as their actions are reasonable and fair regarding the treatment of students.

FREEDOM OF EXPRESSION

Freedom of expression is derived from the First Amendment to the U.S. Constitution, which provides that "Congress shall make no law . . . abridging the freedom of speech, or of press or of the rights of peoples to peacefully assemble."

Stated differently, the First Amendment to the Constitution guarantees the right to freedom of speech to U.S. citizens, including students in public schools. This freedom, however, does not include a license to exercise such rights in a manner that creates *material or substantial disruption to the educational process*. These were the criteria applied by the Supreme Court in determining whether regulations prohibiting student expression were constitutionally valid.

Tinker Case

In 1969, the *Tinker* case emerged as a leading case involving student rights. This case arose when three students wore black armbands to class in protest of the government's policy in Vietnam. They were suspended from school without any evidence that their protest created disruption in school. Interestingly, school officials did not prohibit the wearing of other symbols with political or controversial messages. The students sought a court order to prevent school officials from disciplining them for exercising their First Amendment rights. The U.S. Supreme Court held for the students, stating that it was unconstitutional to discipline students for the peaceful wearing of armbands or other symbols bearing expressions of opinion unless there was evidence of material or substantial disruption to the educational process.

In this landmark 1960s *Tinker* case, the U.S. Supreme Court for the very first time held that *students possess the same constitutional rights as adults and that these rights do not end at the school house door*.[1] This ruling by the high court significantly altered the relationship between school personnel and students. The *Tinker* ruling clearly mandated that professional educators respect the civil rights of students in public schools. In cases where student rights are restricted, school personnel must demonstrate a *justifiable* or *legitimate reason* for doing so. For example, educators may restrict the rights of a student if they are able to demonstrate that such restriction is necessary to maintain order and proper decorum in the school. A student's rights also may be restricted if the exercise of those rights infringes on the rights of others. For instance, a student who delivered a lewd speech at a high school assembly, nominating a friend for a student office, was suspended for three days for using profane language. The U.S. Supreme Court held for the district, stating that the First Amendment does not prevent school officials from disciplining students for indecent speech and protecting other students from vulgar and offensive language.[2] In short, no rights are absolute; rather, they are subject to reasonable restrictions that must be justified by school personnel.

GUIDES

Freedom of Expression

1. School officials may restrict freedom of expression when there is evidence of material and substantial disruption, violation of school rules, destruction of school property, and disregard for authority. In each case, students must be provided minimal due process before any punitive action is taken.
2. Buttons, pamphlets, and other insignia may be banned if the message communicated is vulgar, is obscene, or mocks others based on race, origin, color, gender, or religion. Such items may also be banned if their content is inconsistent with the basic mission of the school. School policies that address these issues should be developed and communicated to students and parents.
3. To justify the prohibition of a particular form of expression, there must be something more than a mere desire to avoid the discomfort and unpleasantness associated with an unpopular view. Such action is arbitrary, capricious, and indefensible.

PROTESTS AND DEMONSTRATIONS

Protests and demonstrations are considered forms of free expression. Therefore, students are afforded the right to participate in these activities under certain conditions. So long as these activities are peaceful, do not violate school rules, and do not result in destruction of school property, protests and demonstrations are allowed. Because school officials are charged with the responsibility to protect the health and safety of all students and to provide an orderly school environment, they may regulate the time, place, and manner of conducting these activities. Such regulations, however, are considered to be mere conditions rather than prohibitions.

School officials should anticipate that minor disruptions, such as noisy and crowded corridors, may occur when there is disagreement or opposite points of view regarding various issues in schools. The courts concur that *minor disruption must be tolerated by school officials.* Only when school officials demonstrate that a particular form of expression has caused or will likely cause material and substantial disruption can they justifiably restrict students' rights to free speech.

GUIDES

Protests and Demonstrations

1. Demonstrations that deprive other students of the right to pursue their studies in an orderly and peaceful environment can be disallowed.
2. Students engaged in demonstrations and protests cannot obstruct the corridors or prevent free movement among students who are not participants in these activities.
3. Any activities associated with demonstrations and protests that result in disrespect for authority, destruction of property, violations of school rules, or any other unlawful activities may be banned.
4. An activity involving students' rights to freedom of expression cannot be banned because it creates discomfort or conflicts with the views of school officials.
5. The time, place, and manner of the distribution of pamphlets, buttons, and insignia may be regulated by school officials. Prohibiting distribution in class during regular school hours or in the corridors between classes is considered reasonable.
6. Unsubstantiated fear and apprehension of disturbance are not sufficient grounds to restrict the right to freedom of expression.

SCHOOL-SPONSORED NEWSPAPERS

Courts generally hold that a school publication has the responsibility for providing a forum for students to express their ideas and views on a variety of topics of interest to the school community. Although the newspaper is intended to represent a forum for student expression, those responsible for its production should be mindful of their obligation to embrace responsible rules of journalism. The school newspaper should reflect editorial policy and sound judgment of student editors who operate under the guidance of a faculty advisor.

Faculty advisors are generally assigned the responsibility to monitor material written for the student newspaper, but, in reality, their primary responsibility should involve advice with respect to form, style, grammar, and appropriateness of material, recognizing that the *final decision for printed material rests with student editors.*

Consequently, student editors, under the guidance of their advisors, should be free to report the news and to editorialize, but at all times adhere to the rules of responsible journalism. A faculty advisor may not be punished, demoted, or dismissed for allowing constitutionally protected material to be printed that may prove distasteful to school officials. When justified, school leaders may exercise *limited review* of school-financed publications so long as they spell out in policy the reason for the review, the time frame involved, the person(s) responsible for reviewing the material, and specifically what material will be reviewed. Students are afforded the right to express their views and ideas that do not materially and substantially affect the operation of the school. Broad censorship by school officials is not permitted and is in violation of the free speech rights of students. In light of these precautions, however, students' free speech rights are not without limits. *Material that is libelous, vulgar, or obscene, or that mocks others on the basis of race, origin, sex, color, or religion, is impermissible.* In cases where the newspaper is produced by students as a part of their school curriculum, school officials may regulate content that is inconsistent with the basic educational mission of the school.

A newspaper produced as a part of the school's curriculum may not enjoy the same privileges as would one that is produced outside of the school's curriculum. Although in both cases the paper is intended to serve as a forum for student expression, more latitude is extended to students when the paper is not considered to be a part of the school's curriculum. For example, if the newspaper is not deemed part of the curriculum, then greater freedom should be granted to student editors in reporting the news when there is no evidence of disruption or defamation. Also, school officials would likely incur less risk of lawsuits if the school's paper is not considered to be a part of the curriculum. However, if it is considered part of the curriculum, then school officials must be allowed to exercise *reasonable control* over newspaper content because they may be subject to liability charges for defamation involving libel.

Although the U.S. Supreme Court's decision in *Hazelwood* provides greater latitude for administrators, courts generally still accept the notion that a school publication has the responsibility for *leading opinions, provoking student dialogue, and providing a forum for a variety of student opinions.*

In a leading case in 1987, the U.S. Supreme Court in the *Hazelwood School District v. Kuhlmeier* reached a landmark decision. Students in a high school journalism course wrote and edited the school newspaper. The principal reviewed the material and deleted two pages containing articles on divorce and teenage pregnancy prior to publication. The Supreme Court ruled that public school officials do not offend the First Amendment by exercising editorial control over the content of student speech in school-sponsored newspapers so long as their actions are reasonably related to valid educational purposes.[3]

GUIDES

Student Newspapers

1. Through the involvement of representative students, teachers, and community citizens, legally defensible policies should be formulated that govern publication of the school's newspaper.
2. Student editors should be chosen who will exercise high standards of responsible journalism.
3. Administrative prerogatives vary based on whether the student newspaper is considered to be an open forum or a curriculum-based publication.
4. Student editors have the primary responsibility to see that the newspaper is free from libelous statements and obscenity. They should be reminded that newspapers are subject to the law of libel.
5. Regulations should be developed that prescribe procedures to be followed in the event that prior review is warranted. These should include:
   a. A definite period of time in which the review of materials will be completed

b. The specific person to whom the materials will be submitted

c. The specific materials that are included for review

CENSORSHIP

Limited review of school sponsored publications may be permitted, but *broad censorship* is not. School officials' commitment to sponsor a student publication should reflect a commitment to respect personal rights associated with freedom of expression. *School officials have the option to decide whether they wish to finance a school-sponsored publication.* Once a decision is made to support an open forum for student ideas, broad censorship powers may not be imposed. School officials must be mindful that students are afforded the right to express their ideas and criticisms when these expressions do not materially and substantially interfere with proper decorum in the school, irrespective of whether the newspaper is considered a part of the school's curriculum or is student sponsored.

GUIDES

Censorship

1. Courts are in disagreement regarding the extent to which school officials may examine and make judgments on student publications prior to their distribution.
2. If prior restraint is invoked, there should be a demonstrated and compelling justification for doing so.
3. School officials must be able to demonstrate that the distribution of a student publication will create a material and substantial disruption.
4. If limited review is legally justified, the following safeguards should be included:
   a. A brief review process
   b. An explanation of the person(s) vested with the authority to approve or disapprove the material
   c. The form in which the material is to be submitted
   d. A clear and specific explanation of the types of items that are prohibited with a rationale as to why they are prohibited
   e. An opportunity for students to appeal the decision if they feel that it is unjust

DRESS AND APPEARANCE

There seems to be a prevailing view that issues involving dress should be left to the decisions of state courts. The U.S. Supreme Court has consistently declined to address this issue. Student dress as a form of free expression is not viewed as significant as most other forms of free expression. There is, however, a First Amendment freedom associated with it.

Dress may be regulated if there is a defensible basis for doing so. However, school regulations that violate students' rights by being vague or ambiguous, and by failing to demonstrate a connection to disruption will not meet court scrutiny. Dress regulations based on fashion or taste as a sole criterion will not survive court scrutiny. School officials, however, may within reason prescribe rules governing student dress and appearance with an emphasis on *reasonableness*. In fact, in some cases, the courts are now requiring school officials to demonstrate the reasonableness of their rules even before they elect to decide if constitutional rights of students are violated.

Dress is generally viewed as a form of self-expression reflecting the student's values, background, culture, and personality. Therefore, restrictions on student dress are justified only when there is evidence of material or substantial disruption to the educational process. Violations of health and safety standards or cases where unusual attention is drawn to a student's anatomy also are justifiable reasons to restrict certain types of dress. The following restrictions have been upheld by the courts regarding dress and appearance:

1. School regulations necessary to protect the safety of students (e.g., wearing of long hair or jewelry around dangerous equipment in laboratories)
2. School regulations necessary to protect health of students (e.g., requiring students to keep hair clean and free of parasites)
3. Rules prohibiting dress that does not meet standards of the community (e.g., dressing in a manner that calls undue attention to one's body)
4. Dress that results in material and substantial disruption to the orderly administration of the school may be prohibited (e.g., wearing T-shirts containing vulgar, lewd or defamatory language based on race, color, gender, sexual orientation, language, national origin, or religion.

Health and Safety Issues

Schools are vested with broad and implied powers designed to protect the health, safety, and welfare of students. Hence, school officials may promulgate reasonable rules and regulations necessary to address health and safety concerns of students. Thus, situations involving certain types of dress that pose a threat to the safety and well-being of students may be regulated. For example, if students are wearing excessively long hair in vocational shop classes or laboratories that pose a threat to their safety, school officials may take appropriate steps to regulate hair length. Also, if jewelry is worn that poses a potential threat to safety where students are engaged in shop, activity-oriented, or physical education classes, similar measures may be taken to regulate the type of jewelry worn.

Students may be required to wash long hair for hygienic purposes. For example, if certain types of fungus are associated with dirty, long hair, a student may be required to take appropriate steps to rectify the problem.

Controversial Slogans

Slogans worn on T-shirts, caps, and other media that are in direct conflict with the school's stated mission may be regulated. Those expressions that violate standards of common decency or that contain vulgar, lewd, and otherwise obscene gestures also may be regulated. In instances where disruption occurs or where there is a reasonable forecast that disruption might occur, school officials may take appropriate action to rectify the situation. These actions are particularly relevant when the content of such expressions mocks others based on race, gender, color, religion, language, sexual orientation, or national origin.

GUIDES

Dress and Appearance

1. Local school dress codes developed by the school should be approved by board of education policies. Faculty, students, parents, and citizens should be involved in the formulation of such regulations.
2. Dress codes will be supported by the courts only when there is evidence that they are reasonable.
3. Dress and appearance restrictions based on taste, style, and fashion rather than health, safety, and order will not pass court scrutiny.
4. Appearance that does not conform to rudiments of decency may be regulated.
5. Dress that is considered vulgar or mocks others on the basis of race, gender, religion, color, language, sexual orientation, or national origin may be prohibited.

SEARCH AND SEIZURE

The Fourth Amendment to the U.S. Constitution provides protection of all citizens against unreasonable search and seizure. This amendment provides in part that "the right of people to be secure in their persons, houses, papers and effects against unreasonable searches and seizures, shall not be violated, and no warrants shall issue, but upon probable cause."

Since students enjoy many of the same constitutional rights as adults, they are granted protection against unreasonable search and seizure. The major challenge facing school personnel involves the task of delicately balancing the student's individual right to Fourth Amendment protection against their duty to provide a safe and secure environment for all students.

To search or not to search a pupil's locker, desk, purse, or automobile on school premises presents a perplexing problem for educators. Basic to this issue is the question of precisely what constitutes a *reasonable search*. The reasonableness of the search becomes the critical issue in cases where students claim personal violations based on illegal searches.

Most authorities point out the distinction between searches of a student's person and those that involve lockers and desks. The major distinction, of course, is that lockers and desks are considered to be school property. Consequently, school personnel are provided greater latitude in searching lockers and desks than they are a student's person.

The underlying command of the Fourth Amendment to the Constitution is that searches and seizures be deemed reasonable. Consequently, if students are to be searched, the search must be reasonable. What, then, constitutes a reasonable search? A reasonable search is one that clearly does not violate the constitutional rights of students. What is reasonable will depend on the context within which a search takes place.

Reasonable Suspicion

School officials and teachers need only reasonable suspicion to initiate a search. This standard is less rigorous than the requirement of probable cause. What exactly constitutes reasonable suspicion? *Reasonable suspicion* is based on information received from students or teachers that is considered reliable. As long as the informant is known rather than anonymous and the information provided seems credible, courts will generally find little difficulty supporting administrative actions based on reasonable grounds.

Consequently, certified school personnel may search if reasonable suspicion is established as the primary basis for the search. The courts have declared that *in loco parentis* (in place of parents) cannot stand alone without reasonable suspicion.

Reasonable suspicion was addressed in the landmark *New Jersey v. T.L.O.* case in New Jersey in 1985, when the Supreme Court reaffirmed that searches conducted by school officials are indeed subject to standards of the Fourth Amendment; however, a warrant requirement in particular is unsuited to the school environment. According to the high court, requiring the teacher to obtain a warrant before searching a child suspected of an infraction of school rules would unduly interfere with the maintenance of the swift, informal disciplinary procedures needed in the schools.

A search of a student by a teacher or school official must be both "justified at its inception" and "reasonably related in scope to the circumstances which justified the interference in the first place." Simply stated, school personnel should have reasonable grounds to believe a search of a particular student is necessary to provide pertinent proof that the student has violated a particular policy, rule, or law. Further, the scope of the search must be limited to the incident at hand. In other words, a sweep search of all students by a teacher in hopes of turning up evidence of contraband or violation of rules would be illegal. There should be individualized suspicion, and *individualized* refers to both the individual student and individual violation.[4] Therefore, indiscriminate searches by teachers are illegal. These types of searches often occur when something of value is missing in the classroom. A search of all students in hopes of locating the missing item is illegal. There has to be specific information that leads the teacher to a particular student or group of students to justify a search of those students.

Student Desks

Student desks are subject to search if the standard of reasonableness is met. Desks should never be searched based on a mere "hunch" but rather, reliable information that leads teachers to believe that school rules have been violated or that health or safety of students is threatened. In all cases, searches should be based on clearly written policies that inform students that desks are subject to search if reasonable suspicion is established. School policies should spell out the conditions and circumstances under which desk searches will occur. Again, wider discretion is provided to educators in searches involving school property.

Student Lockers

School personnel must meet the same standard of reasonableness here as previously mentioned regarding the search of student desks. Because student lockers provide privacy for students, oftentimes there is a greater tendency to expect students to harbor items that violate school rules or items that involve criminal activity. *This view alone does not justify an indiscriminate search.* Again, students should be informed that lockers will be searched if reasonable suspicion is established to justify a need to search. If a search of a student's locker becomes necessary, the student and at least one other school official should be present to ensure that proper procedures are followed. The student affected should open the locker in the presence of school officials. This student may also request the presence of another student if he or she wishes. In no cases except extreme emergencies, such as a bomb threat, should an indiscriminate search be initiated. Barring an emergency, indiscriminate searches of students' lockers are *indefensible* and *illegal.*

Book Bags

Searches involving book bags tend to be extremely complex, due to the intrusive nature of the search itself. A more extensive and intrusive search will likely require stronger evidence to establish reasonable suspicion. At least one court has stated that "we are also of the view that as the intrusiveness of the search intensifies, the standard of Fourth Amendment reasonableness approaches probable cause, even in the school context."[5]

In a 1994 New Jersey case, *Desilets v. Clearview Regional Board of Education,* involving book bag searches of students engaged in a field trip, the Superior Court of New Jersey held that the search of students' hand luggage was justified under the Fourth Amendment, based on a legitimate interest of school administrators and teachers in preventing students from taking contraband on field trips.[6] This decision was supported by the fact that students and parents were informed beforehand that a search would be conducted.

Automobiles

School officials may search a student's automobile parked on school property if the standards of reasonable suspicion are met. Students and parents should be informed by school or district policy that automobiles are subject to reasonable search if there is a legitimate basis for doing so.

If the student's automobile is parked on nonschool property, *probable cause* must be established, involving law-enforcement officials who are required to present a warrant prior to the initiation of a search. Again, parents should be informed of an impending search so as to allow them the opportunity to initiate any steps they deem necessary in this situation. If illegal items such as drugs or weapons are discovered, they are admissible in a court of law.

Personal Searches

Personal searches are strongly discouraged unless there is overwhelming evidence to support the need for the search. Even then, there should be a sense of urgency based on a belief that the student has in his or her possession some dangerous item that could pose a serious threat to the health and safety of the student or others in the school. Whether a search of this nature is considered reasonable will be based on the individual facts surrounding the case. The courts will generally establish the standard based on the facts presented to determine reasonableness. In doing so, the courts will attempt to balance the student's privacy rights against the interest of school officials to conduct the search.

Personal searches of an intrusive nature should be avoided except under extremely serious circumstances. The more intrusive the search, the closer it triggers the need for probable cause. Students should be protected from intrusive body cavity searches if at all possible. When facts reveal that a personal search is necessary, every precaution should be taken to conduct the search in a private setting with persons of the same gender conducting the search. The student should be afforded the greatest amount of protection to privacy as possible under the circumstances. If the search involves removal of a student's garment, the student should be allowed to remove, in privacy, any garments or items of clothing the search warrants. He or she should be provided alternative clothing during the search process.

Only school personnel of the same gender should be involved in this type of search, and extreme caution should be taken to ensure, as much as possible, that the student is not demeaned during this process. Unless there is an extreme sense of urgency, it might be advisable to isolate the student, keep the student under observation, and consult with the student's parents or legal guardian. Under any circumstances, parents should be advised of the type of search conducted, the evidence that gave rise to the need to conduct the search, specifically who was involved in conducting the search, and expressly what was discovered during the search process. Personal searches should be considered searches of *last resort* and should be handled based on school or district policy. They should never be calculated to cause embarrassment or mental distress for the student.

A more intrusive search will require *significant evidence to establish reasonable suspicion and a justification to conduct the search.* Reasonable suspicion must be based on clearly established facts from which rational decisions can be made in order to justify the need to conduct a search.

GUIDES

Search and Seizure

1. A student's freedom from unreasonable search should be carefully balanced against the need for the school to maintain order, maintain discipline, and protect the health, safety, and welfare of all students.
2. Factors such as the need for the search; the student's age, history, and record of behavior; the gravity of the problem; and the need for an immediate search should be considered before initiating a search.
3. A school search should be based on reasonable grounds for believing that something contrary to school rules or significantly detrimental to the school and its students will be produced by the search.
4. The information leading to school searches should be independent of law-enforcement officials. Searches involving law-enforcement officials must be accompanied by probable cause and a search warrant.
5. Although the primary purpose for the search should be to secure evidence of student misconduct for school disciplinary purposes, it may be contemplated under certain circumstances that criminal evidence may be made available to law-enforcement officials.
6. Personal searches should be avoided except where imminent danger exists. Such searches can be justified only in cases of extreme emergency when there is an immedi-

ate threat to the health and safety of students and school personnel. In such cases, school authorities should be certain that their actions are fully justified with convincing information to support this more intrusive search.

7. School personnel should conduct the search in a private setting. At best, a search is a demoralizing experience; care should be taken to minimize embarrassment to the student as much as possible.

8. The magnitude of the offense, the extent of intrusiveness, the nature of the evidence, and the background of the student involved should be considered before a search is initiated.

9. A "pat-down" search of a student, if justified, should be conducted by school personnel of the same gender and with an adult witness of the same gender present, if possible. Personal searches conducted by persons of the opposite sex can be very dangerous.

10. Arbitrary searches or mass shakedowns cannot be justified as reasonable and are illegal.

USE OF PAGERS AND CELLULAR PHONES

The use of pagers and cellular phones by public school students has increased in frequency and popularity in recent years. Students find these devices to be affordable and convenient sources of communication both on and off school premises. Although no legal challenge has reached the courts regarding the school district's authority to restrict or prohibit their use, the courts would likely support school authorities' decision to do so, unless there is evidence that a First Amendment right is in jeopardy, which is unlikely.

It is well established that school officials may prohibit any practice that creates material or substantial disruption to the educational process. School districts may minimize legal challenges when there is evidence that the use of pagers and cellular phones creates disruption or that they are used for improper purposes. School officials are given the authority to maintain a safe and orderly environment to facilitate teaching and learning. Consequently, they may prohibit any practice that affects proper order and decorum, since learning cannot occur in a disruptive environment. When school officials provide evidence that pagers and cellular phones create a disruptive influence in the school and are abused by students, they will likely succeed in prohibiting student possession of these devices on school premises. This prohibition will not likely offend the personal rights of students.

However, school boards, through district policy, may allow special exceptions in cases where such devices are needed for medical emergencies involving students with a chronic illness or other special circumstances that warrant their use. If the use of pagers and cellular phones are prohibited by policy, all allowable exceptions should be filed and readily available should school officials need to retrieve them if challenged by parents who may raise questions regarding preferential treatment. In the absence of compelling evidence that pagers and cellular phones are needed by students, school officials will likely succeed without court intervention so long as they consistently adhere to their own policies and demonstrate no evidence of disparate treatment among students regarding permission to use these devices.

GUIDES

Pagers and Cellular Phones

1. The use of pagers and cellular phones by students should not be banned, unless there is sufficient evidence of disruption or improper use.
2. If permitted, specific guidelines should be developed that govern the conditions under which these devices may be used.
3. If not permitted for general use, exceptions should be allowed, such as cases involving medical emergencies or other special circumstances that warrant the use of these devices.
4. Policies or guidelines should always be guided by a sense of fairness and due consideration for the unique and personal needs of students.

CORPORAL PUNISHMENT

Corporal punishment is a highly controversial issue in the United States today. Perhaps no other issue has drawn as much criticism as the use of physical punishment in public schools. Those who support corporal punishment contend that it will cause changes in student behavior and teach students self-discipline and respect for authority. Those who oppose corporal punishment view it as a legalized form of child abuse, which conveys to students that violence is an acceptable method of resolving problems or disagreements. Irrespective of the views supporting or opposing corporal punishment, the courts still view corporal punishment as an acceptable form of discipline when administered in a reasonable manner. Although corporal punishment is considered an acceptable form of discipline by the courts, school personnel increasingly are facing charges of assault and battery, prosecution, and even termination of employment for abusive acts against students.

Corporal punishment usually involves the use of physical contact for disciplinary purposes. Corporal punishment as a disciplinary tool is not uncommon within school systems in the United States. In fact, 23 states currently allow corporal punishment to be used as a means of discipline. Interestingly, the courts, under the concept of *in loco parentis,* have sanctioned reasonable corporal punishment by school personnel, but there are no laws (except those in one state) that protect school personnel who administer it.*

Southern states have the highest percentage of students receiving corporal punishment, as depicted in Table 4.1. However, the overall number of students struck each year has declined during the past 20 years, with the most dramatic decline occurring in 1997–1998, when school paddlings dropped by 27 percent from the year before, as educators have sought other methods of disciplining students in public schools. Figure 4.1 identifies those states in the United States that have banned corporal punishment.

The question of the constitutionality of corporal punishment was reaffirmed in an important 1977 case, *Ingraham v. Wright,* when the U.S. Supreme Court ruled that even severe corporal punishment may not violate the Eighth Amendment prohibition of cruel and unusual punishment. This case arose when Ingraham and another student from the Dade County, Florida, public schools filed suit after they had been subjected to paddling. State law allowed corporal punishment if it was not "degrading or unduly severe" and if it was done after consultation with the principal or other teacher in charge of the school. Paddling was considered a less drastic form of punishment than suspension. For violating a teacher's instructions, Ingraham received 20 licks while he was held over a table in the principal's office. He required medical attention and missed school for several days.

Because this paddling was probably "unduly severe," the High Court hearing the evidence and appeals found no constitutional violation. According to Justice Powell, "The

---

*The Alabama legislature passed a teacher immunity bill, Act #95-53, that provides immunity for teachers to use corporal punishment or otherwise maintain order when exercising such authority within their local boards.

TABLE 4.1 Corporal Punishment in U.S. Public Schools, 1999–2000 School Year

In the United States as a whole, **342,038** students were subjected to corporal punishment. This is a drop of 7 percent from the previous survey two years earlier [taking enrollment increases into account], continuing a steady trend. Total U.S. public school enrollment was 46,306,355 students in '99–2000. Twenty-seven states and the District of Columbia now have prohibited all corporal punishment in public schools. Data for the remaining 23 states are listed below.

State	Number of Students Hit	Percent of Total Students
Alabama	39,197	5.4
Arizona	632	< 0.1
Arkansas	40,437	9.1
Colorado	260	< 0.1
Delaware	65	0.1
Florida	11,405	0.5
Georgia	25,189	1.8
Idaho	23	< 0.1
Indiana	2,221	0.2
Kansas	99	< 0.1
Kentucky	2,797	0.4
Louisiana	18,672	2.6
Mississippi	48,627	9.8
Missouri	9,223	1.0
New Mexico	2,205	0.7
North Carolina	5,717	0.5
Ohio	1,085	0.1
Oklahoma	17,764	2.9
Pennsylvania	407	< 0.1
South Carolina	3,631	0.5
Tennessee	38,373	4.2
Texas	73,994	1.9
Wyoming	8	< 0.1
U.S. Total	**342,038**	**0.7**

Source: U.S. Department of Education, Office for Civil Rights, 2000 Elementary and Secondary School Civil Rights Compliance Report. Compiled by the National Coalition to Abolish Corporal Punishment in Schools, Columbus, OH 614/221-8829, www.stophitting.com, February 2003.

States that have banned corporal punishment
States that allow corporal punishment
More than half of all students are in districts with no corporal punishment

State	Year	Present Statute
Alaska	1989	Alaska Stat. Section 11.81.430
California	1986	CA Educ. Code Section 49000
Connecticut	1989	CT Gen. Stat. Section 53A–18
Delaware	2003	DE Educ. Code Title 14, Sec. 702
District of Columbia	1977	Board of Education rule
Hawaii	1973	HI Rev. Stat. Section 298–16
Illinois	1993	IL School Code Section 24–20
Iowa	1989	IA Code Section 280.21
Maine	1975	ME Rev. Stat. Section t. 17–a 106
Maryland	1993	MD Educ. Code. Ann. Section 2305
Massachusetts	1971	MA Ann. Laws Ch. 71, Section 37G
Michigan	1989	MI Comp. Laws Section 380.1312
Minnesota	1989	MN Stat. Section 127.45
Montana	1991	MT Code Ann. Section 20–4–02
Nebraska	1988	NE Rev. Stat. Section 79–4, 140
Nevada	1993	NV Rev. Stat. Ann. Section 20–4–302
New Hampshire	1983	NH Rev. Stat. Ann. Section 626:6
New Jersey	1867	NJ Rev. Stat. Section 18A:6–1
New York	1985	NY Penal Law Section 35.10
North Dakota	1989	ND Cent. Code Section 15–47–47
Oregon	1989	OR Rev. Stat. Section 339.250 (8)
Rhode Island		All local boards have banned
South Dakota	1990	SD Codified Laws Section 13–32–2
Utah	1992	UT School Code Section 534–11–802
Vermont	1985	VT Stat. Ann. t. 16 Section 1161a
Virginia	1989	VA Code Section 22.1–279.1
Washington	1993	WA Rev. Code Section 9A.16.100
West Virginia	1994	WV Code Section 81A–5–1
Wisconsin	1988	WI Stat. Section 118.31

Note: Dates listed are when the law was enacted, unless otherwise noted.

Source: Compiled by **Center for Effective Discipline,** 155 W. Main Street, Suite 1603, Columbus, Ohio 43215, tel: (614) 221–8829, www.stophitting.com

FIGURE 4.1   States Banning Corporal Punishment

schoolchild has little need for the protection of the Eighth Amendment." It is more appropriately applied in the case of the criminal convicted and thereby involuntarily confined.[7]

Although the court declined to declare corporal punishment as used in the context of public schools to be a violation of the cruel and unusual proscription or due process under federal law, it did state that paddling students deprived them of liberty interests protected by the Constitution. Although not required by law, but in the spirit of fairness, *rudimentary due process* should be applied prior to its application before corporal punishment is administered. (See Chapter 5 for discussion of due process.) A prudent policy would require that an adult witness be present, and that parents' wishes concerning this form of punishment be considered, if not respected.

Whereas the *Ingraham* case upholds the legality of corporal punishment as an acceptable means of controlling student behavior, local school district policy in many cases has seriously limited its use. Nevertheless, according to a recent survey conducted by the National Center for the Study of Corporal Punishment and Alternatives in Schools, at least two million U.S. schoolchildren are physically punished each year.

Reasonable Punishment

Poor decisions regarding the use of corporal punishment by school personnel may result in civil damage suits or even criminal prosecution for assault and battery. Corporal punishment, when permitted, should be used only as a *last resort* measure. Every reasonable disciplinary measure should be employed prior to its use. Collaboration between teachers, parents, and school officials to resolve a child's deviant behavior is viewed as a more positive alternative.

When corporal punishment is permitted, students should be informed beforehand of specific infractions that warrant its use. When administered, the punishment should be reasonable and consistent with the gravity of the infraction. Corporal punishment should never be administered *excessively* or *with malice*.

In the past, there have been numerous suits alleging that children were struck with double belts, lacrosse sticks, baseball bats, electrical cords, bamboo rods, hoses, and wooden drawer dividers. Other suits have alleged that children were kicked, choked, and forced to eat cigarettes. Such acts by school personnel are totally indefensible. None of these practices meet the test of reasonableness established by today's courts. The right to discipline students is subject to the same standards of reasonableness as would be expected by the average parent.

The courts have advanced two standards governing corporal punishment of students: The first is the reasonableness standard—punishment must be exerted within bounds of reason and humanity. The second is the good faith standard—the person administering the punishment must not be motivated by malice and must not inflict the punishment wantonly or excessively.[8]

Minimal Due Process

The student who is to be punished should be informed of the rule violation in question and provided an opportunity to respond. A brief but thorough *informal hearing* should be provided so as to allow the student the opportunity to present his or her side of the issue. Upon request, parents or guardians must be provided a written explanation of the reasons for the punishment and the name of the school official who was present to witness the punishment.

Excessive Punishment

School officials and teachers must exercise extreme care to ensure that corporal punishment is not deemed excessive. Excessiveness occurs when the punishment is inflicted with such force or in a manner that is considered to be *cruel* and *unusual.* Excessiveness also occurs when no consideration is given to the *age, size, gender, and physical condition, or the student's ability to bear the punishment.*

Assault and battery charges are normally associated with allegations of excessive punishment. Both are classified as intentional torts. An *assault* involves "an overt act or an attempt to inflict immediate physical injury to the person of another. The overt act must be a display of force or menace or violence of such a nature as to cause reasonable apprehension of immediate bodily harm."[9] The person accused of an assault must have the ability to execute it. All of the elements found in this definition must be present to sustain an assault charge. An assault occurs when a person has been placed in fear for his or her immediate safety. A *battery,* on the other hand, is a successful assault that involves actual physical contact.

From the teacher's perspective, when corporal punishment is administered in a rude and malicious manner, using poor judgment regarding the excessive nature of the punishment, assault and battery charges may be eminent, especially if there is a view that the teacher *intended* to harm the student. Intent is an important element involving a battery. The person who inflicts the harm must be perceived as purposely doing so. Although *in loco parentis* allows school personnel to administer corporal punishment, their actions must be considered reasonable and necessary under the circumstances. Corporal punishment should not be inflicted when students resist it. Teachers should be judicious in following school district policy in administering corporal punishment.

GUIDES

Corporal Punishment

1. Corporal punishment should not be used except for acts of misconduct that are so antisocial and disruptive in nature as to shock the conscience.
2. School personnel should not expect the courts to support malicious and excessive physical punishment of students.
3. Reasonable administration of corporal punishment should be based on such factors as the gravity of the offense and the age, size, gender, and physical ability of the child to bear the punishment.
4. If a student professes a lack of knowledge regarding the rule violation or innocence of the rule violation, a brief but adequate opportunity should be provided to explain the rule and allow the student to speak on his or her behalf.
5. Whenever possible, students should be provided punishment options for deviant behavior. Corporal punishment should never be administered when the child is physically resisting.
6. Attempts should be made to comply with a parent's request that corporal punishment not be administered on his or her child, with the understanding that the parent assumes responsibility for the child's behavior during the school day.

CLASSROOM HARASSMENT

Harassment is a form of sexual discrimination. The Supreme Court, in a stunning 5–4 decision, ruled that public schools may be sued for failing to deal with students who harass their classmates.[10] This landmark decision, hailed as a victory by sexual harassment protection groups, raises a number of interesting questions: How will it affect the operation and management of schools? Will it create insurmountable problems of supervision for teachers and principals? Will every adolescent gesture made against a classmate trigger a need for schools to respond? Has the High Court invoked a federal code of conduct that regulates behavior typically associated with adolescence? These are complex issues facing school leaders as they attempt to address harassment issues in their schools.

The Supreme Court's Decision

Justice Sandra Day O'Conner writing for the majority in the *Davis v. Monroe County* case in 1999 involving student to student sexual harassment, attempted to clarify these complex issues by indicating that lawsuits are valid only when the harassing student's behavior is so severe, pervasive, and objectively offensive that it denies the victim equal access to an education guaranteed by federal law. She further suggested that harassment claims are only valid when school administrators are clearly unreasonable and deliberately indifferent toward the alleged harassing conduct which obviously means that they must have been aware of such conduct and did nothing to address it. However, liability charges may be made even if a teacher is the only one aware of the harassing behavior.

GUIDES

Classroom Harassment

1. District policies and procedures should be formulated to address sexual harassment for employees and students. Be certain that everyone—faculty, students, and staff—understands these policies and the consequences for violating them.
2. Educational programs should be provided periodically for faculty, staff, and students to familiarize them with all aspects of harassment and specific behavior considered to fall in the harassment category.
3. Faculty and students should be encouraged to report all violations through a well-defined, developed, and publicized grievance procedure.
4. Educators should react swiftly and judiciously to complaints filed by students so that everyone is clear that the institution considers charges of harassment seriously.

5. An environment should be created where students and school personnel feel comfortable in honestly reporting complaints of harassment free of any form of reprisal.
6. The confidentiality of those filing complaints should be protected to the greatest degree possible. Professional reputations can be damaged if charges prove to be false.
7. A school climate should be created and maintained that is characterized by mutual respect and consideration of others.

CHILD ABUSE

In virtually all states, teachers are required to report suspected cases of child abuse and neglect to the appropriate agency. School districts have procedures for filing these reports. Forty-nine states have mandatory reporting requirements for teachers. If no evidence supports findings of abuse, teachers will not be liable. Immunity is granted in virtually every state when reports are made by teachers in good faith. Laws in most states penalize individuals who fail to report child abuse and neglect. Failure to report abuse is a misdemeanor that generally carries a fine up to $1,000 and a jail sentence.

PREGNANT STUDENTS

The courts have generally held that pregnant students may not be denied the opportunity to attend school. The basis for the court's position is that pregnant students must be afforded equal protection under the law, as well as due process of law.

School officials have attempted to withdraw pregnant students from school based on knowledge that such students have become pregnant, whereas others have specified a particular time for withdrawal. Many of these rules have been successful in the past. However, the courts have become increasingly amenable to declaring these rules invalid. The commonly acceptable practice is that the student's physician may prescribe the time in which the student should withdraw for health and safety reasons. Upon withdrawal, school officials should provide appropriate home-based instruction. When cleared by the attending physician after childbirth, the student may return to school and be entitled to the same rights and privileges afforded other students. A female student cannot be denied participation in school activities, events, or organizations during her pregnancy or after her pregnancy, unless they are disallowed by her physician or school officials can demonstrate a legitimate reason to limit her participation.

MARRIED STUDENTS

Married students have the right to attend public schools. Any rules designed to exclude married students from attending school are invalid and in violation of their Fourteenth Amendment rights—namely, equal protection under the laws. School board rules that prohibited married students from permanently attending public schools were invalidated by the courts during the late 1920s and early 1930s.[11] School rules that required students to withdraw from school for a one-year period after marriage were invalidated by the court.[12] Further, the court established the position that a 16-year-old married student has the right to attend public school, even when she has a child.[13]

Married students are considered *emancipated* and not subject to compulsory attendance laws. Thus, a married or minor student cannot be coerced to attend school. These students may attend as they wish. *Emancipation* means that the student is free of parental authority and control and free to make independent decisions.

There has been debate over the extent to which married students should be permitted to participate in extracurricular activities endorsed by the school. Although extracurricular activities have frequently been viewed as privileges that may or may not be granted by the board, this view has been invalidated on the basis that denying such privileges may violate equal protection and due process provisions of the Fourteenth Amendment. Further, extracurricular activities in most cases are considered to be mere extensions of the regular academic program.

GUIDES

Pregnant and Married Students

1. Pregnant and married students are afforded the same rights as all other students enrolled in public schools, and they may not be prohibited from attending school.
2. There must be compelling evidence to demonstrate that the presence of married or pregnant students creates disruption or interference with school activities or a negative influence on other students to justify any attempt to restrict their attendance.

3. The pregnant student's physician is authorized to determine when the student should withdraw and when it is feasible for her to return.

4. Homebound instruction should be offered for students who have withdrawn due to pregnancy.

5. A heavy burden of proof rests with school officials in instances where attempts are made to exclude either pregnant or married students from participating in regular and extracurricular activities.

6. The courts are unanimous in invalidating school rules that prohibit married or pregnant students from attending school.

ENDNOTES

1. *Tinker v. Des Moines Independent Community School District,* 393 U.S. 503, at 511, 89 S.Ct. 733, 21 L.Ed. 2d 731 (1969).

2. *Bethel School District v. Fraser,* 478 U.S. 675, 106 S.Ct. 3159, 92 L.Ed. 2d 549 (1986).

3. *Hazelwood School District v. Kuhlmeier,* 484 U.S. 260 at 276; 108 S.Ct. 562; 98 L.Ed. 2d 592 (1987).

4. *New Jersey v. T.L.O.,* 469 U.S. 809; 105 S.Ct. 68; 83 L.Ed. 2d 19 (1984).

5. *Bellnier v. Lund,* 438 F. Supp. 47 (N.D.N.Y. 1977).

6. *Desilets v. Clearview Regional Board of Education,* 137 N.J. 585, 647 A.2d 150 (1994).

7. *Ingraham v. Wright,* 430 U.S. 651; 97 S.Ct. 1401; 51 L.Ed. 2d 711 (1977).

8. Ibid., 430 U.S. 651; 97 S.Ct. 1401: 51 L.Ed. 711 (1977).

9. *State v. Ingram,* 237 N.C. 197, 74 S.E. 2d 532 (1953).

10. *Davis v. Monroe County Board of Education,* 526, U.S. 629; 110 S.Ct. 1661; 143 L.Ed. 2d 839 (1999).

11. *McLeod v. State,* 122 So. 77 (Miss. 1929).

12. *Board of Education of Harrodsburg v. Bentley,* 383 S.W. 2d 387 (Tex. 1967).

13. *Alvin Independent School District v. Cooper,* 404 S.W. 2d 76 (Tex. 1966).

five

Due Process and Student Safety

Under the No Child Left Behind Act, school safety has become a major priority for local school districts. Districts must provide assurance that plans are on file regarding the steps schools will initiate to maintain safe and drug-free environments. In March 2003, former Secretary of Education Rod Paige announced that $30 million was available in fiscal 2003 to assist school districts in improving and strengthening emergency response and crises management plans. Additionally, the National School Safety Center (NSSC) was created to provide assistance in combating school safety problems so that schools can be free to focus on the primary job of educating the nation's children. The NSSC was established by presidential directive in 1984 as a partnership between the U.S. Departments of Justice and Education.

CREATING SAFE SCHOOLS

While the nation faces threats of terrorism that affect the health and safety of all citizens, U.S. schools also face safety threats that affect the welfare of students. Maintaining safe schools has become a major challenge for school officials during the past decade. School shootings (in Pearl, Mississippi; West Paducah, Kentucky; Jonesboro, Arkansas; Edinboro, Pennsylvania; Springfield, Oregon; and Littleton, Colorado) have increased pressures on school leaders to provide a safe learning environment where teachers can effectively perform their instructional duties. A survey conducted in the late 1990s by Howard-Met Life revealed a general climate of anger and violence around the nation's schools. A large minority of the student body appears to have a predisposition toward violence based on their inability to control anger. Bullying, insulting, and disrespectful behavior often-times resulted in fights. If access to guns is added, there is a greater probability of violent outcomes. Another major threat to school safety is the presence of youth gangs in schools.

Gang presence in public schools appears to be decreasing. According to a recent report, the percentage of students who reported the presence of street gangs in their schools decreased from 28 percent in 1989 to 17 percent in 1999. Although gang presence has decreased, it still poses a major challenge for school leaders.

With the presence of gangs in schools, school leaders are encountering pressures from parents, citizens, and school boards to provide a safe environment where teachers can teach and students can learn. Added to these pressures is the court's view that schools are "safe places" based on the assumption that children are supervised by licensed and well-trained teachers and administrators. Since schools are presumed to be safe, failure to provide a safe environment can prove costly when evidence reveals that school leaders failed to act responsibly in protecting students when they knew or should have known of impending danger.

Youth join gangs for various reasons, including the desire for excitement, peer pressure, neglect, economic reward, lack of appropriate involvement elsewhere, and the need for recognition, identity, and acceptance. They show strong loyalty to their gang and will do whatever is necessary to be initiated into the gang, including committing violent crimes. In some cases, the lack of success in school and a feeling of alienation contribute to gang affiliation.

Gangs are forces that are challenging schools and communities across the nation. School leaders, however, have an especially important role to play, since gang violence has quickly become a part of public schools' vocabulary.

GANGS AND DRESS

Gang members tend to wear specific apparel or colors to convey gang affiliation. Where gang activity has been prevalent in the school or community and there is clear knowledge that certain types of dress are associated with disruptive gang activity, school leaders may prohibit such dress. In all cases, such prohibitions should be preceded by school policies that clearly communicate the need to regulate this type of dress.

In most cases, the pattern or style of dress is generally chosen by gang leaders. As pressure is exerted by parents, law-enforcement officers, and school officials, gangs will often change their appearance to become less recognizable. Today, many gang members wear professional sports team jackets, caps, and T-shirts, making it difficult to identify them. Since school officials are responsible for protecting students from potential danger, they may take reasonable steps to minimize gang presence in school. Conversely, school officials should provide opportunities for all students to succeed in school and to feel that they are important members of the school's family.

GUIDES

Gangs and Dress

1. Efforts should be made to ensure that school personnel have knowledge of gang identification strategies as well as gang management techniques.
2. Policies and procedures should be established to address gang violence in the school.
3. A system should be implemented to report suspected gang involvement and activity to proper law-enforcement gang units.
4. Dress related to gang activity may be banned by school officials.

School Uniform Dress Policies and Students' Freedom of Expression Rights

Many school officials, in their desire to create and maintain safe schools, have developed uniform student dress code policies. These policies are intended to provide easy identification of students, eliminate gang dress, promote discipline, deter theft and violence, prevent unauthorized visitors from intruding on campus, and foster a positive learning environment. Although there is no consensus regarding the effectiveness of school uniforms, their use is increasing in schools across the nation as part of an overall program to improve school safety and discipline.

Early Legal Challenges

With frequent acts of violence in public schools, school districts are moving swiftly and aggressively to enforce uniform dress policies. Early legal battles have already surfaced over dress codes and religious freedoms in Mississippi, involving the rights of students to wear clothing with religious symbols to school. Officials in Harrison County, Mississippi, backed off on the same day of enforcing a regulation that prohibited a Jewish student from wearing a Star of David necklace to class based on its policy of prohibiting students from wearing anything that could be viewed as a gang symbol. A similar case arose in Van Cleave, Mississippi, when a local board of education banned students from wearing clothing with Christian symbols based on the school's mandatory uniform policy. In this case, two students wore T-shirts stamped with the words *Jesus Loves Me.* The basis for implementing the mandatory uniform policy was safety. After an unsuccessful appeal to the school board, parents of the two students filed a suit in U.S. District Court, challenging the legality of a policy that prohibits free expression of their children's religious freedom. These early legal cases may suggest a lack of some degree of sensitivity to the First Amendment rights of students as school uniform policies are drafted.

GUIDES

Uniforms

1. Parents, teachers, community leaders, and student representatives should be involved in drafting school uniform policies.
2. Students' religious expressions must be protected in relation to uniform dress codes.
3. Students' freedom of expression rights should be protected within reasonable limits as uniform dress standards are established.
4. School uniform policies should be enforced fairly and consistently.
5. School uniform policies should be implemented as a component of an overall school safety program.
6. School uniform policies should be reviewed and revised as the need arises.

ZERO TOLERANCE AND SCHOOL SAFETY

School safety has become a leading priority for school leaders across the nation as they respond to a wave of violence that has struck public schools throughout the United States, resulting in 348 deaths between 1992 and 2003. Although schools are still considered safe places, limiting violence has quickly become a major challenge for school officials. Many districts have initiated a zero tolerance policy in an effort to reduce school violence. Opponents are raising questions as to whether school leaders are going too far and moving too swiftly with a "one strike you're out" approach. They also are questioning whether school leaders' actions are reasonable and legally defensible.

Recent Zero Tolerance Practices

Since zero tolerance has emerged in a number of districts, students have been affected in ways that raise questions regarding the legal defensibility of these approaches. For example, a 16-year-old female student in Washington was met by police and expelled for using her finger to make a gun and jokingly stating, "Bang." She has since been reinstated. A 13-year-old male student in Texas was arrested and spent five days in jail awaiting a hearing for writing an unsettling story about killing classmates. He is currently receiving home schooling. An 18-year-old male student in Georgia wrote a story in his journal about a deranged student who goes on a rampage at school that resulted in expulsion and arrest with no opportunity to graduate. Other accounts involve a 7-year-old who was suspended for bringing nail clippers to school in Illinois.

Unquestionably, school officials are relatively uneasy about school safety based on past incidents of violence in schools. However, their concerns must be tempered with sound reason and a regard for the rights of students. Policies that do not weigh the severity of the offense, the student's history of past behavior, due process, or alternative education for students involved in long-term expulsion are at best highly risky. Although most of the incidents cited did not reach the courts, the case involving the account of a deranged student did. In this case, the judge ruled that the student's journal entry did not, in fact, constitute a threat. Even with the judge's ruling, the student had to switch schools. Prosecutors are still weighing a case against him.

GUIDES

Zero Tolerance

1. Zero tolerance policies should not be used solely to rid the school of disruptive students.
2. Teachers, parents, community leaders, and student representatives should be involved in the formulation of zero tolerance policies.

3. Policies should be formulated with the recognition that students possess constitutional rights.
4. Zero tolerance should not be considered a cure-all for student misconduct.
5. When it becomes necessary to expel students for an extended period of time, alternative educational opportunities should be sought.
6. The student's history of behavior in school, the seriousness of the offense, and the immediate need to act should be considered before determining punishment.
7. The student's substantive and procedural process rights should be safeguarded in all disciplinary matters.

SCHOOL SUSPENSION

School suspension is considered a legal form of discipline for students who violate school or district policy. In-school suspensions are used by a number of school districts in the United States. However, out-of-school suspensions remain the most prevalent. Race, ethnicity, and socioeconomic status are often factors that impact school suspensions based on a study by the Applied Research Center, a nationally based research education and policy institute in Oakland, California. There appears to be a close relationship between socioeconomic status, race, and ethnicity and the rate of suspensions. Larger numbers of minority students are suspended yearly who typically occupy lower socioeconomic status than that of their peers.

School suspensions require that *procedural* and *substantive* provisions of due process be met. Basically, due process is a course of legal proceedings following established rules that assure enforcement and protection of individual rights. The guarantees of due process require that every person be entitled to the protection of a fair hearing. The essential element of due process is *fundamental fairness,* which means a fair hearing, and a fair, impartial judgment.

GUIDES

School Suspension

1. Adequate notice must be provided to students and parents regarding the existence of rules governing student behavior. These should be clearly communicated to all affected by their implementation.

2. A record should be compiled that includes the following information:
   a. The infraction allegedly committed
   b. The time of the alleged infraction
   c. The place the alleged infraction occurred
   d. The person(s) who witnessed the alleged act
   e. Previous efforts made to remedy the alleged misbehavior
3. Students should be provided either oral or written notice of charges against them, the evidence school authorities have to support the charges, and an opportunity to refute the charges.
4. Since permanent removal is not intended, no delay is necessary between the time notice is given and the time of the actual hearing. In most instances, informal discussion by school officials regarding alleged misconduct may be discussed with students immediately after it is reported.
5. During the hearing, the school official should listen to all sides of the issue. There should be adequate time provided for students to present their side of the issue without interruption.
6. Parents or guardians should be informed of the hearing and provided written notification of the action that results from the hearing.

Procedural and Substantive Due Process

Due process consists of two essential aspects: procedural and substantive. Students as citizens are entitled to rights associated with both aspects. *Procedural due process* requires that certain legal procedures be followed to ensure fundamental fairness and to avoid arbitrary and capricious actions by school officials, whereas *substantive due process* deals with the student's individual or personal rights.

Substantive due process suggests that when a student's rights are restricted, a valid reason must be demonstrated to justify such restriction and the actual means employed to deny the student's right must be reasonably calculated. Procedural due process requires that a *legally defensible procedure* be followed to ensure that proper safeguards are available to protect the rights of those whose rights are in jeopardy. The significance of substantive and procedural requirements is that both provisions must be met by school officials to succeed in meeting the basic requirements of the Fourteenth Amendment.

EXPULSION

Unlike suspension, expulsion is considered one of the more severe forms of discipline because it involves long-term separation from the school district and in some instances permanent separation. Expulsion usually involves more serious offenses or rule violations than does suspension. In recent years, a significant number of expulsions have been linked with weapons violations. For example, in 2004 alone, more than 6,000 U.S. students were expelled for bringing weapons to school. These numbers represent only 29 states and the District of Columbia. With increased gang presence in school, and frequent incidents of violence, student expulsions will continue to escalate.

Expulsion is typically used by school districts as a form of discipline for students who commit serious infractions. Since expulsion is considered to be a form of discipline that deprives the student of the right to attend school, it must be preceded by a formal due process hearing in which the student is afforded full Fourteenth Amendment rights involving due process and equal protection privileges.

Because the threat of expulsion is so serious, students and parents should be aware of the types of infraction that may result in expulsion. These infractions should be identified by school and district policy. Additionally, they should be clearly communicated to students and parents to ensure that there is no misinterpretation regarding the intent and substance of expulsion policies.

Parents, students, community citizens, and school personnel should be involved in the development of expulsion policies, recognizing that the board of education has the ultimate authority for approving such policies.

In virtually every state, the board of education is the only body with legal authority to expel students. The board is responsible for holding the expulsion hearing and meeting all rudiments of due process consistent with the Fourteenth Amendment. Any errors along procedural or substantive grounds usually will result in the student being supported by the courts.

GUIDES

Expulsion

1. Students and parents or legal guardians should be informed of school or district policy of specific infractions

that may result in expulsion. They should also be informed of their Fourteenth Amendment rights regarding substantive and procedural due process.

2. In cases of serious misconduct for which serious disciplinary measures may be imposed, the student is entitled to written notice of the charges and a right to a fair hearing. Written notice must be furnished to the student and parent or guardian well in advance of the actual hearing.

3. At a minimum, the following procedural steps should be considered:
   a. Written notice of charges
   b. Right to a fair hearing
   c. Right to inspect evidence
   d. Right to present evidence on student's behalf
   e. Right to legal counsel
   f. Right to call witnesses
   g. Right to cross-examination and confrontation
   h. Right against self-incrimination
   i. Right to appeal

METAL DETECTORS

Metal detectors have grown in use and popularity as school officials seek to maintain a safe and orderly school environment. To date, there has been no legal challenge reaching the Supreme Court regarding the use of detectors. However, litigation has occurred at the district court level. In the *Thompson v. Carthage School District* case in 1996, a school bus driver reported fresh cuts in a seat cushion and reported it to the principal who ordered that all male students in grades 6 through 12 be searched based on school policy. There also was information indicating that drugs were present in the school. The students were searched using metal detectors. One student was searched and crack cocaine was found. He was subsequently expelled. The student filed suit, alleging wrongful expulsion. The district court ruled for the student. However, the appeals court reversed the district court's decision by indicating that the exclusionary rule compromises school safety and held that the search was justified from its inception based on reasonable suspicion and inferences.[1]

The use of metal detectors, like other intrusive methods, must be justified as reasonable and necessary to meet a legitimate school objective. In this case, maintaining a safe and orderly school environment was considered a legitimate school objective. There should be, in all cases, *significant* or *compelling evidence* to suggest that metal detectors be used. If a school has a chronic history of drug use and violence involving the use of weapons, the courts will likely support the use of metal detectors as a means of combating these problems. If metal detectors are employed by the school officials, students should be informed before the procedure is implemented that they are subject to this type of screening. Such information should be included in school or district policy and clearly communicated to students and parents. In no instance, except extreme emergencies, should students be surprised by the use of metal detectors. Also, if detectors are used, the methods employed in using them must be reasonable and not designed to degrade students.

GUIDES

Metal Detectors

1. Metal detectors should be used only when there is evidence of student behavior that poses a threat to the health and safety of students in the school. Students and parents should be informed beforehand that metal detectors will be employed and the basis for employing this method, barring an emergency situation.
2. If metal detectors are used to achieve a legitimate school interest, its use will likely be supported by the courts.
3. Students and parents should be informed through a legally defensible school policy regarding the use of metal detectors.
4. If school officials' acts are reasonable regarding the use of metal detectors, they will generally receive support of the courts.

DRUG TESTING

Until the mid-1990s, no case involving drug testing in public schools had been litigated by the U.S. Supreme Court. The *Veronia School District v. Acton,* however, reached the Supreme Court in 1995 when the Ninth Circuit Court reversed the district court's holding for the school district. School officials in Oregon formulated a district policy based on the belief that some athletes had been smoking marijuana and using other drugs. They also believed that drugs were a major factor in the formulation of rowdy student groups. Under the district's policy, all student athletes were required to provide a urine sample at the beginning of the season for the particular sport in which they participated. Athletes who tested positive were offered the choice to undergo counseling and weekly testing or to face suspension from athletics for the current and subsequent season. This policy was challenged by a prospective athlete.

The Supreme Court held that the Vernonia School District's program was reasonable and constitutionally permissible for three reasons. First, students, especially student athletes, have low expectations for privacy in communal locker rooms and restrooms where students must produce their urine samples. Second, the testing program was designed to be unobtrusive, with students producing their samples in relative privacy and with the samples handled confidentially by an outside laboratory. Finally, the program served the district's interest in combating drug abuse.[2] Some courts have recently supported random drug testing programs for students involved in other extracurricular activities.

ALCOHOL USE AND BREATHALYZERS

School districts should develop policies aimed at discouraging alcohol use by students. The policy should be sufficiently definite so as to inform students of expectations regarding alcohol use on school property or any school-sponsored event. School officials should exercise caution and avoid conducting random testing of students. Such practice would be considered arbitrary, capricious, and indefensible.

A breathalyzer test should be used only when reasonable suspicion has been established that points to either a single student or a group of students who are thought to be under the influence of alcohol. Even then, care must be exercised to ensure that breathalyzer tests are conducted in privacy and not in a manner that creates embarrassment for the student.

Breathalyzer policies should be designed to deter students from the use of alcohol. An alcohol education course would be valuable in informing students of the health risks associated with alcohol use as well as risks associated with becoming dependent on alcohol. A teacher has the responsibility to report any student whom he or she believes is under the influence of alcohol. School officials should investigate using school or district policy for guidance in conducting breathalyzer tests.

GUIDES

Drugs and Alcohol Testing

1. A districtwide program on drug education and alcohol abuse should be initiated, stressing the harmful effects of drugs and abstention from the use of drugs.

2. School and district policies should be developed prohibiting the use and/or possession of drugs on school grounds, indicating specific actions that will be taken when students are found guilty of violating school and district policy.

3. A full due process procedure should be implemented to ensure that there is a fair and impartial opportunity for student athletes to present their side of the issue, if accused of drug use.

4. Teachers, parents, student athletes, health officials, and community citizens should be involved in formulating school and/or district policies regarding drug testing programs that are reasonable and legally defensible.

5. Support should be provided in cases where students are found guilty of drug use. This is a time when students need as much support as possible.

6. Open relationships should be maintained with parents so that frequent communication can occur, especially in cases where there is a suspicion that a student may be involved with drugs.

ENDNOTES

1. *Thompson v. Carthage School District,* U.S. App. Lexis 15461 (8th Cir. 1996).
2. *Veronia School District v. Acton,* 115 S.Ct. 2386; 132 L.Ed. 2d 564 (1995).

six

Liability and Student Records

The primary purpose of maintaining educational records should be to aid school personnel in developing the best educational program for each student enrolled in the school. An effective student file contains information used for counseling, program development, individualized instruction, grade placement, college admissions, and a variety of other purposes. In addition to certain types of directory information, student files typically include family background information, health records, progress reports, achievement test results, psychological data, disciplinary records, and other confidential material.

Public Law 93-380, the Family Educational Rights and Privacy Act (FERPA), protects confidentiality of student records. This act, commonly referred to as the Buckley Amendment, was enacted by the Congress in 1974 to guarantee parents and students a certain degree of *confidentiality* and *fundamental fairness* with respect to the maintenance and use of student records. The law is designed to ensure that certain types of personally identifiable information regarding students will not be released without parental consent. *If a student is 18 years of age or attends a postsecondary institution, parental consent is not required.* In that event, the student has the authority to provide consent. If the student is a dependent for tax purposes, parents retain a co-extensive access right with students over 18 years old.

Because P.L. 93-380 is a federal statute, it applies to school districts and schools that receive federal funds. Schools should develop policies and procedures including a listing of the types and locations of educational records and persons who are responsible for maintaining these records. Copies of these policies and procedures should be made available to parents or students upon request.

SANCTIONS FOR VIOLATING FAMILY PRIVACY RIGHTS

An excerpt of the Family Educational Rights and Privacy Act states the following:

> *No funds shall be available under any program to any educational agency or institution which has a policy of denying access or which effectively prevents the parents of students who are or have been in attendance at a school of such agency, the right to inspect and review the educational records of their children. If any material or document in the educational record of a student includes information on more than one student, the parents of one of such student shall have the right to inspect and review only such part of such material or document as related to such student or be informed of the specific information contained in such part of such material.[1]*

At a minimum, the school district should provide, on an annual basis, information to parents, guardians, and eligible students regarding the content of the law and should inform them of their rights to file complaints with the Rights and Privacy Act Office of the Department of Education. If non-English-speaking parents are affected, the district has a responsibility to notify them in their native language.[2] Annual notification must include the following information:

1. The right to inspect and review educational records
2. The right to seek amendment of records believed to be inaccurate, misleading, or in violation of the student's privacy
3. Consent to disclose personally identifiable information contained in the student's records except where the act authorizes disclosure without consent
4. The right to file with the department a complaint under § 99.63 and 99.64 concerning alleged failures by the educational agency or institution to comply with requirements of the act
5. A notice including the following:
   a. Procedures for exercising the right to inspect and review educational records
   b. Procedures for requesting amendments of records

    c. Specification of criteria for determining who constitutes a school official and what constitutes a legitimate educational interest

6. A notice by an educational agency or institution effectively notifying parents or eligible students who are disabled

7. A notice by an educational agency or institution of elementary and secondary education effectively notifying parents who have a primary or home language other than English

Additionally, parents, guardians, and eligible students should be provided information regarding procedures for accessing educational records, if they desire to do so. The content of education records is shown in Table 6.1.

The school district may release directory information regarding students, provided that such information is published yearly in a public newspaper. Directory information normally includes:

1. Name
2. Address
3. Telephone number
4. Date and place of birth

TABLE 6.1 Content of Educational Records

Educational Records Include	Educational Records Do Not Include
1. Records	1. Instructional records
2. Files	2. Supervisory records
3. Documents	3. Records maintained by law-enforcement units for law-enforcement purposes
4. Other material that: a. contains information directly related to a student b. is maintained by an educational agency, institution, or person acting for agency of institution	4. Records on an 18-year-old student attending a postsecondary institution that are maintained by a physician, psychiatrist, psychologist, or other recognized professional or para-professional involved in the treatment of the student

Source: P.L. 93–380.

5. Participation in extracurricular activities
6. Weight, height, and membership on athletic teams
7. Dates of attendance
8. Diploma and awards received

If any parents or guardians object to the release of directory information on their child, their objection should be noted in the record and honored by the school district. School policy should define what items are considered directory information and the conditions under which this information should be released.

Except for directory information, all personally identifiable records directly related to the student shall be kept confidential, unless the parent or guardian signs a consent form releasing certain such information.

Rights of Parents

Parents or legal guardians have the right to inspect their child's school record. A school official should be present to assist a parent or guardian in interpreting information contained in the files and to respond to questions that may be raised during the examination process. Parents or legal guardians may challenge the accuracy of any information found in the files regarding their child. The school must schedule a conference within a reasonable period of time (10 or fewer days, although the act calls for no more than 45 days) with appropriate personnel to discuss the information, which may be deemed inaccurate, inappropriate, or misleading. If agreement is reached to the satisfaction of the parent, no further action is necessary. Appropriate deletions or corrections are executed, recorded in the student file, and communicated to parents or guardians in written form.

If the conference does not result in changes to the satisfaction of parents, they may request a hearing with the Director of Pupil Personnel or a designee to appeal the decision reached during the conference. The hearing should be scheduled within 10 or fewer days. The parent or guardian may be represented by legal counsel. A final decision should be rendered within 10 days subsequent to the hearing. If the school official hearing the case decides that the information is accurate and correct, the parent must be informed of such and provided an opportunity to place statements of disagreement in the file with reasons for the disagreement. This explanation must become a permanent part of the record and must be disclosed when the records are released. The parent or guardian may also seek relief in civil court.

When consent is necessary to release student records, it must be provided in written form and signed and dated by the consenting person. The consent form should include a specification of the records to be released, reason for the release, and the names of the individuals to whom the records will be released. Once records are received by the requesting party, it should be emphasized that this information is not to be divulged to other parties without the expressed permission of the parents, guardians, or eligible students. *Parents, guardians, or eligible students must be notified before a school or district complies with a judicial order requesting educational records.* School officials in another school district in which a student plans to enroll may access that student's records, provided parents or guardians are notified in advance that the records are being transferred to the new district.

Rights of Noncustodial Parents

Occasionally, controversy arises regarding the rights of a noncustodial biological parent to access his or her child's educational records. School officials often find themselves caught between a custodial parent's request that the noncustodial parent not be permitted to access the child's educational records. School or district policy should provide guidance in these situations. Such a case occurred in New York when the mother of a child requested that the school not allow the child's father to see their son's educational records. The father challenged the school's refusal to allow him access to the child's records. The district court ruled that neither parent could be denied access to the child's records under the Family Educational Rights and Privacy Act. The court held that schools should make educational records accessible to both parents of each child fortunate enough to have both parents interested in the child's welfare.[3]

Rights of Eligible Students

As previously mentioned, the student may exercise the same rights afforded parents or guardians, if he or she has reached the age of 18 or is enrolled in a postsecondary institution. The student may inspect confidential records and also challenge the accuracy of information contained in the file. Additionally, the student may determine whether anyone other than authorized individuals may have access to his or her personal files. All students also have the right to receive a copy of their personal file, if they choose to have one. Eligible students are afforded the same due process provisions as parents are offered, if they choose to challenge the accuracy of information contained in their file. They may also, under certain conditions, bring liability charges for defamation against school personnel (discussed later in this chapter).

Rights of School Personnel

Teachers, counselors, and administrators who have a legitimate educational interest in viewing records may do so. A written form, which must be maintained permanently with the file, should indicate specifically what files were reviewed by school personnel and the date in which files were reviewed. Each person desiring access to the file is required to sign this written form. These forms should be available for parents, guardians, or eligible students, since they remain permanently with the file. If challenged, school personnel must demonstrate a legitimate interest in having reviewed a student's file.

In 1994, FERPA was amended to emphasize that institutions are not prohibited from maintaining records related to a disciplinary action taken against a student for behavior that posed a significant risk to the student or others. Likewise, institutions are not prevented from disclosing such information to school officials who have been determined to have a legitimate educational interest in the behavior of the student. School districts also are permitted to disclose information regarding disciplinary action to school officials in other schools that have a legitimate educational interest in the behavior of students.

Table 6.2 summarizes the rights of all parties affected by FERPA.

Enforcement of State or Federal Statutes

Federal officials and state officials may inspect files without parental consent in order to enforce federal or state laws or to audit or evaluate federal education programs. In these cases, personally identifiable information may not be associated with any student unless Congress, by law, specifically authorizes federal officials to gather personally identifiable data. Information may also be released without consent in connection with applications for student financial aid. Authorized representatives who may access records include (1) the Comptroller General of the United States, (2) the Secretary of State, (3) an administrative head of an educational agency, and (4) state and educational authorities. School district policies should address these issues so that parents, guardians, and eligible students are informed of these exceptions.

TABLE 6.2 Rights under FERPA

Rights of Students (for students who are 18 years old or who attend a postsecondary school)	Rights of Parents	Rights of School Personnel
1. Have knowledge of types of records and location of records and inspect confidential educational records	1. Inspect child's record if under age 18	1. Access to confidential information for legitimate educational purposes
2. Challenge the accuracy of information contained on records	2. Challenge the accuracy of information contained on records	2. Maintain personal notes about students for personal use
3. Have appropriate deletions or corrections executed	3. Have appropriate deletions and corrections executed	3. Disclosure of educational records to comply with judicial orders for state and various federal agencies
4. Hearing to contest information on records thought to be inaccurate	4. Hearing to contest information on the records thought to be inaccurate	4. Disclosure of disciplinary proceedings conducted against alleged perpetrators of a crime
5. Consent to disclosure of personally identifiable information contained in files	5. Place statements of disagreement regarding contested information remaining on the records	5. Disclosure of directory information on students

(continued)

TABLE 6.2   *(Continued)*

6. Determine what type of confidential information is released and to whom other than those authorized to access confidential information	6. Determine what type of information is released and to whom it is released other than authorized personnel and reasons to be released	6. Privilege against lawsuits when making truthful statements in good faith within the scope of professional duties
7. Place statements of disagreement regarding any contested information remaining on the records	7. Receive annual notice of rights under the act	7. Record truthful negative information on education records that should remain a part of the permanent record
8. Receive a copy of personal records	8. Receive prior notice of any records subpoenaed by the courts	8. Receive training on handling sensitive and confidential information on students with disabilities
9. Receive a copy of released record upon request	9. File complaints with the U.S. Department of Education concerning alleged violations	9. Receive protection when factual references of students are provided when requested
10. Under certain conditions, bring charges of defamation against school personnel and other appropriate parties	10. Seek relief in civil court if necessary	10. Destroy records when no longer needed after student graduates

Source: P.L. 93–380.

RECENT U.S. SUPREME COURT RULINGS ON FERPA

On February 19, 2002, the U.S. Supreme Court ruled in *Owasso ISD v. Falvo*[4] that peer grading does not violate FERPA. The Department of Education has reviewed the Court's ruling and may issue additional guidance or regulations to further clarify the scope of the term *education records*.

DEFAMATION INVOLVING SCHOOL PERSONNEL

Defamation regarding liability applies to student records. When teachers communicate personal and sensitive information to another unauthorized person that results in injury to the student's reputation standing in the school, or that diminishes the respect and esteem to which the student is held, they may face charges of *libel* or *slander,* depending on the manner and intent in which such information was communicated.

Defamation is a tort or civil wrong. It occurs when false statements are made about another person with the intent to harm a person's good name and/or reputation, or to subject the person to hatred, contempt, or ridicule.

Slander

Slander is oral defamation that occurs when school personnel inadvertently communicate sensitive and damaging information contained in student files to others who have no need to be informed. Libel and slander involve communication to a third party. Information contained in student files is there for the exclusive use of the teacher, principal, and counselor, all of whom have a legitimate interest in accessing this information as each works with the student. Information should not be accessed without meeting this requirement.

Once the information is ascertained, it should be used only in providing and improving educational opportunities for the student. By no means should confidential information be discussed in a canny and joking manner. Under no circumstances should the student be ridiculed. The law is very specific in indicating that personally identifiable information should not be communicated to third parties without proper consent. When this is done, not only has the law been violated but the educator has also run the risk of defaming the student. Off-the-cuff remarks and sharing sensitive information regarding a student's personal file is absolutely prohibited and may result in liability damages to those who are guilty of committing this act.

School personnel are well advised to maintain strict confidentiality in all cases involving students' personal files. In cases involving claim of personal injury, the burden of proof rests with the student in demonstrating that actual harm occurred based on deliberate communication to a third party.

Libel

Libel, unlike slander, is written defamation. Teachers, counselors, and principals should refrain from including damaging information in a student's record for which there is no basis. Any information recorded should be factual and specific with respect to serious infractions committed by the student—for example, time and place in which infractions occurred and possible witnesses who might verify, if needed, that the incident described is an accurate account of what actually occurred.

Another consideration involves a determination as to whether certain types of information should be included in a student's permanent file. Some legal experts feel that information that is subject to change and minor disciplinary infractions should be maintained in a separate file and destroyed after the student leaves school. For example, if there is no evidence of serious and recurring behavior problems, one might question the wisdom of including a single occurrence on the student's permanent records. On the other hand, if there is a strong belief that the behavior is sufficiently serious that it needs to be passed on to those who will be working with the student in the future, it might be appropriate, under the circumstances, to do so. Sound and rational judgment is required in these cases. These decisions must be carefully drawn, due to the serious implications involved. When it becomes necessary to record a serious disciplinary infraction on the student's record, it should be executed in the presence of the student who should be provided a copy of the document.

School personnel should refrain from statements that are based on opinion, particularly those involving questions of *morality, contagious diseases, family marital conditions, and mental or emotional issues.* These statements are damaging, based on their content and, if communicated to others, may result in injury to a student's reputation, self-esteem, or standing in the school. Categorical statements or stereotypical statements should be avoided. If educators adhere to confidentiality and respect for the privacy rights of students, they will avoid liability claims involving injury to students.

Professionalism and ethics dictate that these practices be followed.

Privilege

On many occasions, school personnel are requested to provide either oral or written information regarding a student, some of which might be contained in the student's file. When such requests are made and school personnel respond in a truthful and reasonable manner in accordance with their prescribed duties, they are protected by *qualified privilege*. When school personnel and the recipient of the information both have a common interest, they also are protected by a qualified privilege when the communication is reasonable to achieve their objective. Those who have common interest would likely include counselors, subject-matter teachers, administrators, and parents. Interestingly, this privilege is lost if the communication is transmitted to another who does not share this common interest and consequently has no need to be apprised of the information.

Good Faith

Qualified privilege is based on the premise that the educator is operating in *good faith*. When damaging or sensitive information is communicated to others who have no need to know, good faith has been violated. Good faith requires that a legitimate purpose be served by communicating the information. Common interest in the student's well-being would constitute a legitimate purpose. Good faith efforts dictate that as information is shared with other eligible parties, it is communicated for legitimate purposes and without any intent or desire to damage the student. An absence of good faith may result in personal damages against those who do not operate in a reasonable and prudent manner.

Acts of Malice

Malice exists when there is intent to harm or injure another. Intent is an important element regarding malicious behavior. When statements are communicated regarding a student, either written or oral, with the intent to injure his or her reputation, a tortious act has occurred, especially if these statements are false. *Truth* is a defense for liability, if no malicious intent is present. School personnel should exercise care in ensuring that statements communicated to others are free of malice, based on defensible evidence, and communicated in a professional, nonbiased, and truthful manner. When evidence reveals that school personnel acted in *bad faith* with the *intent* to injure a student's reputation and standing the school or community, liability charges may be justified even if the statements are true. Students are entitled to a *liberty right* with respect to the expectation that their reputation will be protected against unwarranted attacks.

There are essentially two types of malice. In *implied malice,* the offender has no defense for conveying harmful information. Such statements normally fall in the category of unsolicited or derogatory statements aimed at another person. In *actual malice,* the person offended must demonstrate that the person making the offensive comment had a motive for doing so and that this motive was calculated to generate ill will against the offended person. Both types may create serious legal problems for school personnel.

Educators should be very careful not to invoke opinions about students that might be damaging without having the qualifications to make such statements. Any statements regarding another's mental, psychological, or emotional status are very risky; hence, these types of statements should be avoided. Educators should provide only reasonable information based on good faith for which they are qualified to make. Even though truth is a defense against defamation claims, it is not absolute. If statements are made about another that will automatically result in injury to that person's reputation, truth will not be a reasonable defense in this situation. Statements, although true, involving marital status, sexual preference, or contagious diseases may result in defamation charges if persons against whom these statements are made can prove that they were damaged.

CONFIDENTIALITY ISSUES INVOLVING SCHOOL COUNSELORS

A number of states have passed laws protecting the confidentiality of counselors, but most states do not support confidentiality protection for counselors. Michigan and Nevada have the most complete protection. States such as South Dakota, Ohio, Maine, Oregon, Alabama, Arkansas, Idaho, Indiana, Kentucky, Missouri, Montana, North Carolina, Oregon, and Pennsylvania provide protection to counselors in civil and criminal proceedings. However, most communication between a school counselor and a student does not rise to a civil or criminal proceeding. In states where no privilege is granted, the counselor is required to testify if ordered by the court.

In the school setting, counselors are not required to share information obtained from students with their parents. Records that remain in the sole possession of counselors are not subject to FERPA. Educational records under FERPA do not include personal files of counselors. Confidentiality, however, is not absolute. When circumstances arise in which public disclosure is in the public interest, confidentiality is lost. One of the most significant examples occurred in *Tarasoff v. Regents of the University of California* in 1976 in which during a therapy session a student confided to his psychologist that he was going to kill another student.[5] Tatiana Tarasoff was subsequently killed by the student. Her parents filed suit, claiming that the psychologist had a duty to warn their daughter and them of an impending danger. The psychologist did, however, inform campus police. The California Supreme Court ruled that the psychologist had a duty to warn the victim. Further, the psychologist became sufficiently involved to assume some responsibility for the safety not only of the patient but also of any person whom the psychologist knew to be threatened by the patient.

GUIDES

Liability and Student Records

1. School districts and schools should have legally defensible policies and procedures consistent with the requirements of FERPA. Students, parents, and legal guardians should be informed of their rights under this act.
2. Accurate records should be maintained in the student's file indicating the name, title, date, description of educational interest, specific records examined, and the place of examination of student records for those who have access.
3. Any corrections or adjustment to student records should be dated and initialed by the person responsible, with the knowledge and approval of school officials.
4. School personnel should avoid labeling children in ways that damage the student's self-esteem.
5. When it becomes necessary to place disciplinary infraction information on student records, the information should be specific regarding the infraction committed—

time, place, and witnesses, as appropriate. The student should be present when such information is recorded.

6. Teachers should refrain from aimless chatter involving third parties regarding confidential information found on student records. Gossip or careless talk among school personnel calculated to harm a student is not protected by qualified privilege.

7. Student records should be maintained in a safe and secure place and should not be removed from school premises by school personnel unless proper authorization is secured.

8. Unless prohibited by court order, the noncustodial parent should be afforded the same right to access student records as the custodial parent.

9. Releasing information over the telephone should be avoided, unless identity of the other party has been firmly established.

10. Public disclosures of students' grades will not likely be supported by the courts. Such practices violate the intent of FERPA and should not be supported by school officials.

ENDNOTES

1. 20 USC S. 1232 g.
2. C. F. R. § 99.6.
3. *Page v. Rotterdam-Mohonasen Central School District,* 441 N.Y.S. 2d 323 (Sup. Ct. 1981).
4. *Owasso Independent School District No. 1–011 v. Falvo,* 534 U.S. 426; 122 S.Ct. 934; 151 L.Ed. 2d 896 (2002).
5. *Tarasoff v. Regents of the University of California,* 17 Cal.3d 425; 551 P.2d 334; 131 Cal. Rptr. 14 (1976).

seven

Individuals with Disabilities

In 1975, Congress enacted *P.L. 94-142, the Education for All Handicapped Children Act,* based on findings that supported the need for the act. Congress discerned that there were more than eight million children in the United States with disabilities whose educational needs had not been fully met. Roughly four million of these same children had not been provided appropriate educational services, which allowed them to receive an equal educational opportunity. Even more startling was the realization that over one million children with disabilities had not received any type of public educational opportunity. Many of those who did receive some form of public education were not able to receive the full benefits of an educational experience because their disabilities had not been discovered. In many instances, parents were forced to seek assistance for their child with disabilities outside the public school arena, oftentimes at great expense and inconvenience to the family.

Based on these findings, Congress realized that it was in the nation's best interest for the federal government to intervene and work collaboratively with states in addressing the needs of children with disabilities throughout the country. This intervention was presented in the form of P.L. 94-142. The Education for All Handicapped Children Act (EAHCA) has undergone a number of amendments since its inception. As of 1990, it has been referred to as *Individuals with Disabilities Education Act (IDEA).* Although the act has been amended on a number of occasions, its primary purpose has remained intact.

There has been a steady increase in the number of children who have been classified with disabilities. This growth trend highlights the importance of the need to continue to improve services to meet the need of children with disabilities and provide equal access to educational opportunities.

Individuals with disabilities are protected by three significant federal statutes: the Individuals with Disabilities Education Act of 1990 (IDEA), the Americans with Disabilities Act of 1990 (ADA), and the Rehabilitation Act of 1973, Section 504. These statutes were enacted to protect individuals with disabilities from discrimination and to provide them equal access to educational opportunities, facility utilization, and employment opportunities in public school settings.

INDIVIDUALS WITH DISABILITIES EDUCATION ACT OF 1990 (IDEA)

Mandatory Requirements

As stated previously, IDEA succeeded Public Law 94-142 to the Education of All Handicapped Children Act of 1975. Congress passed the IDEA to clearly define the responsibilities of school districts regarding children with disabilities and to provide a measure of financial support to assist states in meeting their obligations.

The IDEA essentially guarantees a child with disabilities, ages *3 to 21*, the right to a free, appropriate education in public schools. This statement also establishes *substantive* and *procedural due process rights* for disabled students. To meet eligibility requirements, a state must develop a plan to ensure a free, appropriate education for all children with disabilities within its jurisdiction. Additionally, each state must formulate a policy that ensures certain due process rights for all children with disabilities. The state's plan should include its goals and a timetable for meeting these goals, as well as the personnel, facilities, and related services necessary to meet the needs of children with disabilities. The state's plan also must include a well-designed system for allocating funds to local school districts. In turn, each local district must submit an application to the state, demonstrating how it will comply with the requirements of IDEA. District plans must be on file and available for review by citizens upon request.

The IDEA requires each state to allocate federal funds first to children with disabilities who are not receiving any type of education and subsequently to children with the most severe disabilities within each disability category. The IDEA further stipulates that, to the fullest extent possible, children with disabilities must be educated with children having no disabilities. In principle, no child with disabilities may be excluded from receiving a free, appropriate public education. The statute does not require such a child to demonstrate that he or she will benefit from special education as a condition to receiving educational services. With the wide array of disabilities, the IDEA does not require equality of results; it merely requires that children with disabilities benefit from instruction.*

Functional Exclusion of Children with Disabilities

Two practices tend to create additional challenges for children with disabilities: exclusion from educational programs and misclassification based on improper assessment. Both practices may result in functional exclusion of children with disabilities. *Functional exclusion* occurs when children with disabilities receive a highly inappropriate placement which denies them an opportunity to receive an appropriate education. Both of these practices will generally result in legal challenges. In recent years based on IDEA, considerable progress has been made regarding inclusion of students with disabilities. Unfortunately, errors continue to occur regarding proper classification and placement. Consequently, school officials should exercise caution to ensure that classification and placement of children with disabilities are executed properly.

Interpretation and Identification of Children with Disabilities

The term *children with disabilities* is defined by the IDEA as those who meet the following conditions:

> *Mental retardation, hearing impairments which include deafness, speech or language impairment. visual impairment including blindness, learning disabilities, brain injury, emotional disturbance, orthopedic impairments, autism, traumatic brain injury, specific learning disabilities and other impairments who by reason of such conditions need special education and related services.*[1]

---

*Reauthorization of the IDEA is currently in progress, which may produce changes to some components of the statute—namely, in the areas of increased funding, attorneys' fees for school districts involved in frivolous lawsuits, paperwork reduction, and services for homeless/foster children among others.

Prereferral Intervention

Regular classroom teachers have the responsibility of identifying students who may need special services in order to receive the full benefits of an education. This function should be executed before any formal assessment or special programming occurs. In short, the teacher must raise the question after carefully working with the student over a reasonable period of time and examining the student's work to determine if the student needs special assistance beyond that which is provided in the regular classroom. This question should emerge after continuous and multiple efforts have failed to meet the needs of the student through the regular classroom program. Deficiencies in academic performance, as well as those related to social and interpersonal behavior, may be evident during the teacher's work with and observation of the student.

After the regular classroom teacher has worked with a student and appears convinced that the student needs special assistance, a request should be made in the form of a *referral*. Virtually all school districts have well-developed policies and procedures regarding referrals. Although the procedures vary from district to district, usually there is some type of referral form used by the regular teacher when a student is deemed to need special services. This form should be as inclusive as possible in providing relevant information needed to conduct a formal assessment of the student if needed. Data requested on the referral form may include the student's name, present grade level, age, gender, standardized test scores, local test data, strengths and weaknesses in key subject areas, reading ability, behavior and relationships with fellow students, pertinent family data, and teaching methods or strategies that have been successful, as well as those that have been unsuccessful.

If a formal assessment procedure is contemplated, the student's parent must grant consent and be informed of personal rights under due process procedures. Teachers should approach the referral process with great care, since it impacts the student's education, consumes time and district resources, and may result in stigmatizing a student.

It is not uncommon for districts to hold prereferral conferences to discuss concerns regarding the student's academic and social performance. These meetings will usually involve the referring teacher, a special education professional, the principal, the counselor, and, in many instances, the parent. Such meetings might be used as an intermediate measure to discuss the implementation of new and different strategies regarding the student's academic and social performance. During this time, an evaluation period should be established to assess the student's progress before a formal assessment is contemplated and decisions made regarding the need for special services. It is highly desirable to employ some type of intervention prior to implementing a formal assessment process. This measure, if implemented appropriately, may reduce *overreferrals and misclassifications,* and result in the best education program for the student, particularly when new strategies and interventions are implemented and evaluated over a reasonable period of time.

The school's review process should be consistent with state and federal regulations. If it is determined that the student's problem stems from a disability, a classification is agreed upon during the conference in which the parent is present. Once the classification is agreed upon, this information is passed on to a committee that, along with the parent, will engage in developing the student's individualized educational program (IEP). The parent must sign the IEP and approve any placement outside of the regular classroom.

School districts are required to evaluate every child with disabilities to determine the nature of the disability and the need for special education and related services. Prior to this evaluation, each district must forward to the child's parent a written notice, in the parent's native language, describing the proposed evaluation process. Parental consent must be sought prior to the actual evaluation. If consent is not provided, the district must initiate an impartial hearing through a hearing officer to secure approval to conduct the evaluation.

Once approval is granted, the evaluation must be fully objective and free of any form of bias. It should be conducted in the child's native language by a multidisciplinary team qualified to assess a wide range of skill areas. Every effort must be made to ensure that only validated tests designed to assess specific areas of need are utilized. This evaluation process should occur in a timely fashion and address each area of the child's suspected disability.

No single test should be used as the sole criterion for determining disabilities, but rather a battery of appropriate tests designed to assess areas of suspected disabilities. The child's strengths and weaknesses should be identified during this process, since these will determine to a large extent the nature of his or her individualized program. A parent or legal guardian who is dissatisfied with the evaluation may secure an independent evaluation at the school district's expense, unless the hearing officer agrees with the district's assessment. In either case, reevaluation of each child with disabilities should minimally occur every three years.

Individualized Educational Program Requirement

When the evaluation results are produced, an individualized educational program (IEP) must be designed for each child with disabilities. This process usually involves one or more meetings in which the child's teacher, parent, and special education representative for the district are present to review and discuss evaluation results. It is also recommended that a representative from the evaluation team be present to respond to questions and interpret results. If feasible, this person may be represented by the child's teacher or the special education supervisor. At a minimum, each individual educational program should include the following:

1. A statement detailing the child's present level of educational performance
2. A statement of annual goals as well as short-term instructional objectives
3. A description of specific educational services to be provided and a determination as to whether the child is able to participate in regular educational programs
4. A description of transitional services to be rendered if the child is a junior or senior in high school to ensure that necessary services are provided when the child leaves the regular school environment
5. A description of services to be provided and a timetable for providing these services
6. An explanation of relevant criteria and procedures to be employed annually to determine if instructional objectives are or have been achieved
7. An annual review of the student's IEP and modifications as needed

Least Restrictive Environment

The IDEA embraces the notion that children with disabilities be placed in educational settings that offer the least amount of restrictions, when appropriate. This view is supported by the philosophy that children with disabilities should be educated with children having no disabilities under normal classroom conditions. The primary objective is to provide the child with disabilities an opportunity to interact, socialize, and learn with regular students, thus minimizing the tendency to become stigmatized and isolated from the school's regular program. There is also inherent value in providing students without disabilities an opportunity to increase awareness of the many challenges faced by children with disabilities and to sensitize them to their unique needs. Therefore, the least restrictive provision of the act mandates the inclusion of students with disabilities into regular classrooms.

This regulation is designed to ensure that students with disabilities be provided the broadest range of opportunities, based on the least restrictive environment provisions. The interpretation of precisely what constitutes the least restrictive environment has led to conflicts as well as litigation. Generally, when a child with disabilities is not involved in regular classroom instruction, the district must demonstrate through the evaluation and IEP process that a segregated facility would represent a more appropriate and beneficial learning environment. Because the law indicates a strong preference for inclusion, the burden of proof rests with educators to demonstrate that their decisions are not arbitrary or capricious regarding the placement of the child with disabilities. The statute does not mandate inclusion in each case involving children with disabilities, but it does require that inclusion be used to the fullest extent possible and as appropriate based on the unique needs of the child with disabilities.

The least restrictive environment (LRE) is a relative concept. What constitutes the least restrictive environment for one child might be totally inappropriate for another. Because there is such wide variation of needs among students with disabilities, there is no ideal way to provide appropriate educational services to such children. Given the variations among these students, a range of placement options must be provided, which might include but not limited to the following possibilities:

- Regular class with support from regular classroom teachers
- Regular class with support instruction from special teachers
- Regular class with special resource instruction
- Full-time special education class in regular school
- Full-time special school
- Residential school
- Homebound instruction

The particular placement options should be determined by the needs of the child who has disabilities and the type of environment that will best meet his or her educational and social needs.

Under the concept of inclusion, regular classroom teachers in schools across the country are challenged to meet the needs of students with disabilities. In many instances, they are unprepared to do so. Since the IDEA specifies that students with disabilities be provided a free, appropriate public education in the least restrictive environment based on the student's individualized educational program, there is an affirmative obligation placed on schools to serve the needs of students with disabilities. If teachers are not prepared to meet these needs, a legal issue may emerge regarding both *academic injury* as well as *physical injury* to the student with disabilities.

With increasing frequency, regular classroom teachers are called on to meet the academic needs of students with disabilities and to perform related services such as *catheterization, suctioning, colostomy, and seizure monitoring when students with disabilities are placed in regular classrooms.* If they are unable to perform these vital services effectively, resulting in injury to the child with disabilities, liability charges may be forthcoming, depending on the nature of the injury and factors leading to such injury. Thus, classroom teachers are often expected to meet the academic needs of children with disabilities and, in most cases, provide special education services during the inclusion period.

Equal Access to Assistive Technology for Students with Disabilities

The Technology-Related Assistance for Individuals with Disabilities Act Amendments of 1994 provides financial assistance to states to support systems changes that assist in the development and implementation of technology-related support for individuals with disabilities. The act further ensures timely acquisition and delivery of *assistive technology devices* including equipment and product systems commercially acquired, modified, or customized that are used to increase, maintain, or improve functional capabilities of a child with disabilities.

Technology assistive services are also included in this act and involve any service that directly assists a child with a disability in the selection, acquisition, or use of an assistive technology device. These services may include:

1. Purchasing, leasing, or otherwise providing for the acquisition of assistive technology by the child with disabilities

2. Selecting, designing, fitting, customizing, adapting, applying, maintaining, repairing, or replacing assistive technology devices
3. Coordinating and using other therapies, interventions, or services with assistive technology devices such as those associated with existing education and rehabilitation plans and programs
4. Training or technical assistance for the child with disabilities or, when appropriate, the family of such child
5. Training or technical assistance for professionals (including individuals providing education and rehabilitation services), employers, and other individuals who provide services to or who are otherwise substantially involved in the major life functions of such child

Program Review and Changes

As previously stated, each IEP must be reviewed and revised annually, if necessary, to ensure that the continuing needs of the child are met. When changes are contemplated, the child's parent or legal guardian must be notified. If the parent or guardian objects to the proposed changes, an impartial hearing must be held to resolve the conflict. If this process proves unsuccessful, the parent or guardian may appeal to the state agency and subsequently to the courts if a resolution is not reached at the state level. This appeals process is designed to ensure fundamental fairness and to meet the requirements of due process, as spelled out in the Individuals with Disabilities Education Act.

Education-Related Service Requirement

A *related service* is viewed as one that must be provided to allow the child with disabilities to benefit from special education. A related service may be a single service or an entire range of services or programs needed to benefit the child. Examples of such services include, but are not limited to, the following: *transportation, medical services, counseling services, psychological services, physical therapy, speech pathology, audiology, occupational therapy, and medical services.*

Inclusion of Children with Disabilities

Inclusion is an extension of the traditional concept of *mainstreaming*. Its intent is to ensure, as much as possible and when appropriate, that children with disabilities be placed in regular classrooms. Inclusion is seen as one mechanism designed to ensure that children with disabilities receive a free, appropriate education in an effort to maximize their learning potential.

Implicit in this concept is the view that some educational benefit is conferred on students with disabilities when they attend public schools. A child's evaluation results, which are used to develop the IEP, would ultimately determine the nature of the placement. Since the IEP is tailored specifically to meet the needs of the child with disabilities, it must be reasonably calculated to enable the child to receive the benefit of instruction.

Inclusion also is valuable in integrating children with disabilities into the regular school program. Many educators feel that both groups—children with and without disabilities—benefit from this arrangement. Although many educators support inclusion as a mechanism to place the children with disabilities in the most ideal educational environment, there are many others who feel that inclusion places these children in nonsupportive environments, eliminating valuable time from their learning activities. This may be particularly critical in environments where the classroom teacher is not properly trained to work with children who have disabilities. The preparation of teachers to meet the needs of these children is critical, since inclusion is an important component of the IDEA that supports equal access for children with disabilities.

Attention Deficit Hyperactivity Disorder and Federal Protection

A growing number of children with attention deficit hyperactivity disorder (ADHD) are enrolled in public schools. Three federal statutes—the Individuals with Disabilities Education Act (IDEA), Section 504 of the Rehabilitation Act of 1973 (RHA), and the Americans with Disabilities Act (ADA)—cover children with attention deficit hyperactivity disorder.

Under IDEA, ADHD-eligible students must possess one or more specified physical or mental impairments and must be defined as requiring special education and related services based on these impairments. Attention deficit hyperactivity disorder alone is not sufficient to qualify a child for special education services, unless it impairs the child's ability to benefit from education. Children with ADHD may be eligible for special education services if they are found to have a specific learning disability, be seriously emotionally disturbed, or possess other health impairments.

Section 504 of the Rehabilitation Act provides education for children who do not fall within the disability categories covered under IDEA. This statute further requires that a free, appropriate public education be provided to each eligible child who is disabled but who does not require special education and related services under IDEA. *A free, appropriate education,* as defined under Section 504, includes regular or special education and related services designed to meet the individual needs of students consistent with the provisions involving evaluation, placement, and procedural safeguards.

DISCIPLINING STUDENTS WITH DISABILITIES

It has long been held that children with disabilities may not be punished for conduct that is a *manifestation* of their disability. However, students with disabilities may be disciplined by school personnel for any behavior that is not associated with their disability by using regular disciplinary procedures, as reflected in school policies. In situations where certain types of discipline are warranted, an effort must be made to ensure that the punishment does not *materially* and *substantially* interrupt the child's education. School suspensions, transfers, and expulsion are examples that fall into this category.

Expulsion

Children with disabilities are neither immune from a school's disciplinary process nor are they entitled to participate in programs when their behavior impairs the education of other children in the program. School officials may exercise at least two options in this situation. First, school authorities can take swift disciplinary measures, such as suspension, against disruptive children who have disabilities. Second, a Planning and Placement Team (PPT) can request a change in placement to a more restrictive environment for children with disabilities who have demonstrated that their present placement is inappropriate by disrupting the education of other children. The Disabilities Act thereby affords schools with both short-term and long-term methods of dealing with children with disabilities who are behavioral problems.

Schools may use their normal disciplinary procedures to address behavior of students with disabilities—if that behavior is nondisability related. As ruled in the *S-1 v. Turlington* case in 1981, school authorities may not discipline students with disabilities for behavior that is a manifestation of their disability.[2]

Since certain types of disciplinary measures may involve removal of children with disabilities from their placement, caution must be exercised to ensure that proper procedural guidelines are followed. As established in an early case, *Stuart v. Nappi,* in 1978, suspension of a student with disabilities is tantamount to a change in placement, thus triggering the "stay put" provision of the IDEA.[3] These decisions may involve transfers, suspensions, and expulsions. The "stay put" provision of the IDEA requires that children with disabilities remain in their current placement, pending the completion of the individualized educational placement (IEP) review process.

When there is agreement between the parent and school authorities, the child remains in the current placement, even though it may not be deemed the most appropriate one at that time.[4]

If either the parent or school authorities wish to temporarily change the placement before the appeals process is exhausted, a *court order* must be ascertained to affect this change. If a decision is reached that a child's placement should be changed, special education and related services cannot be discontinued. The child must receive educational support.

Suspension

School suspension is one of the most common forms of punishment used to remove disruptive students from the school environment. It is particularly useful as a disciplinary tool in cases where there is an immediate threat to health and safety of the child with disabilities or other children in the school. A temporary suspension may be justified in cases that fall into this category. There has been considerable disagreement among school authorities regarding the limits of their authority to temporarily remove children with disabilities in emergency situations when health and safety of students are threatened.

In a compelling case, *Honig v. Doe,* in 1988, the U.S. Supreme Court responded to this issue. This case involved two emotionally disturbed students who had been suspended indefinitely for violent conduct related to their disabilities pending the results of an expulsion hearing. Both students filed suit, contending that the suspensions and proposed expulsions violated the "stay put" provision of the IDEA. The district court ruled for the students and the ruling was later affirmed by the Court of Appeals. The case was reviewed by the U.S. Supreme Court. The fundamental issue confronting the High Court was whether the "stay put" provision of the act prohibits states from removing children with disabilities from school for violent or disruptive conduct stemming from their disabilities. The court reasoned that states may not remove students with disabilities from classrooms for violent or disruptive conduct stemming from their disability under the act.

Schools, however, may use their normal procedures in dealing with students who endanger themselves or others. Students who pose an immediate threat to school safety may be temporarily suspended for up to 10 days without inquiring into whether the student's behavior was a manifestation of a disability. This type of suspension, consistent with an earlier case, *Goss v. Lopez,* involving students without disabilities, is considered to be a short-term suspension, which allows school authorities the freedom to punish a student with disabilities by removing the student from the classroom in anticipation of further action that might involve long-term suspension, movement to a more restrictive environment, or, as a last resort, expulsion.

The significance of this ruling is that the High Court does not interpret short-term suspension as a change in placement and therefore does not trigger the need for elaborate procedural requirements associated with the Act.[5] However, it is important to note that long-term suspensions and expulsion do constitute a change in placement and may not be used if the conduct of the student with disabilities is associated with a known disability. Under the Individuals with Disabilities Education Act of 1997 Amendments regarding discipline, a student may be placed in an *interim alternative education setting (IAES)* for up to *45 days* provided, however, that the same sanction is used for students without disabilities. This sanction applies if the student carries a weapon to school or to a school function, or illegally uses drugs or sells or solicits the sale of a controlled substance at school or at a school function. (For weapons/drug discipline, "stay put" does not apply.)

Congress has approved the reauthorized Individuals with Disabilities Education Improvement Act. President George W. Bush signed this act into law; most provisions of the Act take effect July 5, 2005. Table 7.1 provides a summary of the major changes under the new reauthorization act.

GUIDES

Students with Disabilities

1. School districts should ensure that children with disabilities in their districts be provided equal access to a public education. Failure to provide appropriate special education may result in a court injunction as well as mandatory compensatory education.

2. A well-organized and coordinated staff development plan should be generated to prepare all teachers to work effectively with children who have disabilities. These activities should be coherent, continuous, and well supported by the district.

3. School personnel should be aware of potential liability challenges if they fail to perform certain related services properly.

4. Parental rights must be respected and addressed in matters relating to evaluation and IEP development.

5. Children with disabilities should not be disciplined for behavior that is associated with their known disability.

6. Long-term suspension, if necessary, will trigger the need for change of placement requirements, but in virtually no cases should children with disabilities be without educational services. School officials should become familiar with the new IDEA amendments regarding discipline of students with disabilities and be certain that they are incorporated into district policy.

7. The burden of proof rests with the school district in determining whether misbehavior by a student with disabilities is attributed to his or her disability.

8. According to one court, school districts are expected to provide sign language interpreters at district expense to deaf parents of hearing children at school-initiated activities related to the academic or disciplinary aspects of the child's education.

9. School districts may be required to provide educational services beyond the regular school year, depending on the unique needs of the student with disabilities.

ENDNOTES

1. 20 U.S.C. §1400 (C) (1988).
2. *S-1 v. Turlington,* 635 F. 2d 343 (5th Cir. Unit B Jan). Cert. denied, 454 U.S. 1030 (1981).
3. *Stuart v. Nappi,* 443, F. Supp. 1235 (D. Conn. 1978).
4. 20 U.S.C. §1415 (1997).
5. *Honig v. Doe,* 484 U.S. 305, 108 S. Ct. 592 (1988).

TABLE 7.1 Summary of Major Changes under the Reauthorized IDEA 2004 P.L. 108-446

Section	Heading
Sec. 602(1)(B).	*"Assistive Technology."* Added that term does not include surgically implanted medical device or replacement of such a device.
Sec. 602(4).	*"Core Academic Subjects."* Defined "Core Academic Subjects" as English, reading and language arts, mathematics, science, foreign languages, civics and government, economics, arts, history, and geography.
Sec. 602(10).	"Highly Qualified." 1. Added the requirements for All Special Education Teachers— a. All special education teachers come under NCLB definition (sec. 9101); *PLUS, special education teachers must* b. Have State special education certification OR have passed State licensing exam AND have license to teach special education; c. Have not had certification or licensure waived on emergency, temporary, or provisional basis; AND d. Have at least a bachelor's degree.
Sec. 602(18).	*"Limited English Proficient."* Added the definition from NCLB (Sec. 9101): An individual, aged 3–21, enrolled or preparing to enroll in an elementary or secondary school, 1. a. who wasn't born in the U.S. or whose native language isn't English; b. who is a Native American or Alaska Native, or native resident of the outlying areas and comes from an environment where a language other than English has significantly impacted level of English language proficiency; or c. who is migratory, with native language other than English, from an environment where a language other than English is dominant; and 2. whose difficulties in speaking, reading, writing, or understanding English may be sufficient to deny the child a. ability to meet proficient level of achievement on State assessments; b. ability to successfully achieve in class where instruction is in English; or

(continued)

TABLE 7.1 *(Continued)*

	c. opportunity to participate fully in society.
Sec. 602(36).	*"Ward of the State."* Added new definition—A child who, as determined by State of residence, is a foster child, ward of the state, or in custody of a public child welfare agency. Does not include foster children whose foster parents meet IDEA "parent" definition.
Sec. 602(26).	*"Related Services."* Added "school nurse services" and "interpreting services."
Sec. 602(34).	*"Transition Services."* Added that services must be focused on improving academic and functional achievement, and that the student's strengths must also be taken into account.
Sec. 602(35).	*"Universal Design."* Added definition from the Assistive Technology Act of 1998 (Sec. 3)—"A concept or philosophy for designing and delivering products and services that are usable by people with the widest possible range of functional capabilities, which include products and services that are directly usable (without requiring assistive technologies) and products and services that are made usable with assistive technologies."
Sec. 607.	*"Requirements for Prescribing Regulations."* Public comment period is changed to not less than 75 days. Regulations are limited only to those necessary to ensure compliance with requirements of the law.
Sec. 608.	*"State Administration."* States must notify LEAs and the Secretary in writing of any State rules, regulations, or policies not required by federal law or regulation. States must minimize the number of such rules, regulations, or policies, and those issued must be designed to enable students to meet academic achievement standards.
Sec. 609.	*"Paperwork Reduction."* Authorized a 15-State pilot authorizing waivers of Part B statutory or regulatory requirements to reduce "excessive paperwork and non-instructional time burdens" that do not improve students' educational or functional results.
Sec. 611(e)(3).	*"Local Educational Agency Risk Pool."* States may opt to reserve annually 10% of funds reserved for State-level activities to establish a

TABLE 7.1 *(Continued)*

	high cost fund and to support innovative ways of cost sharing.
Sec. 612(a)(3).	**"Child Find."** Added that "homeless children" and "wards of the State" who may be children with disabilities in need of special education and related services must also be identified, located, and evaluated.
Sec. 612(a)(14).	**"Personnel Qualifications."** Special education teachers must be highly qualified by the NCLB deadline (not later than the end of the 2005–06 school year). Language regarding 3-year waiver to meet highest standard has been eliminated. Instead, the State must adopt a policy that requires LEAs to take "measurable steps to recruit, hire, train, and retain highly qualified personnel."
Sec. 612(a)(16).	**"Participation in Assessments."** Added the following: 1. *All* children with disabilities participate in *all* assessments, with accommodations and alternate assessments as indicated on the IEP. 2. State, or, for district-wide assessments, the LEA guidelines must provide for alternate assessments aligned with the State's academic content and achievement standards.
Sec. 612(a)(21).	**"State Advisory Panel."** The following new members have been added: an official responsible for carrying out the McKinney-Vento Homeless Assistance Act and a representative of the State child welfare agency responsible for foster care.
Sec. 612(a)(23).	**"Access to Instructional Materials."** States must adopt the National Instructional Materials Accessibility Standard (NIMAS) to provide instructional materials to blind persons or those with print disabilities.
Sec. 612(a)(24).	**"Overidentification and Disproportionality."** State adopts policies and procedures designed to prevent inappropriate identification or disproportionate representation by race and ethnicity of children as children with disabilities.
Sec. 613(a)(9).	**"Records Regarding Migratory Children with Disabilities."** LEA works with the Secretary under NCLB (Sec. 1308) to provide electronic

(continued)

TABLE 7.1 *(Continued)*

	exchange among States of health and educational information on migratory children.
Sec. 613(f).	*"Early Intervening Services."* An LEA may use up to 15% of its federal allotment annually, in combination with other funds, to develop and implement coordinated early intervening services for students, grades K–12 (focusing on K–3), who have not been identified as needing special education and related services, but need extra academic and behavioral support to succeed in the general education environment.

Sec. 614(a)(1)(b).	*"Request for Initial Evaluation."* Changes include:
	 1. Initial Evaluation:
	  a. Either parents or the SEA, other state agency or LEA may request an initial evaluation.
	  b. Eligibility determination must be made within 60 days of receiving parental consent for evaluation, or, if the State has an established timeframe for evaluation, that timeframe may be used.

Sec. 614(b).	*"Evaluation Procedures."* Changes and additions include: 1. Conduct of Evaluation: a. Assessments must be provided and administered in "the language and form most likely to yield accurate information on what the child knows and can do academically, developmentally, and functionally. . . ."
Sec. 614(d)(1)(A).	*"Individualized Education Programs."* Added: IEP must include a statement, beginning not later than the first IEP in effect when the student is 16 and updated annually, of "appropriate measurable postsecondary goals based on age appropriate transition assessments related to training, education, employment, and where appropriate, independent skills." Will also include transition services, including courses, needed to assist in reaching goals, contained previously in the age 14 transition requirement.
Sec. 614(d)(1)(C), (D); 614(3)(D)–(F).	*"IEP Team Attendance, IEP Team Transition; Meetings."*

TABLE 7.1 *(Continued)*

	1. IEP team attendance: a. A team member is not required to attend a meeting if parents and LEA agree that member's attendance is not necessary because the member's curriculum area or related service will not be discussed.
Sec. 614(d)(2)(C).	***"Program for Children who Transfer School Districts."*** 1. Transfer within the same State: If a child with an IEP in effect transfers to another school district within the State during the school year, new LEA shall provide FAPE, including services comparable to the previous IEP, in consultation with parents, until new LEA adopts the previous IEP or develops and implements new IEP. 2. Transfer outside State: If a child with an IEP in effect transfers to a school in another state during the school year, new LEA shall provide FAPE, including services comparable to the previous IEP, in consultation with parents, until new LEA conducts evaluation, if deemed necessary, and develops new IEP.

Sec. 615(i).	***"Administrative Procedures."*** Changes and additions include:
	 1. Civil Action: A party bringing a civil action shall have 90 days from the date of hearing officer's decision to bring an action, or, if the State has an explicit time line, shall follow the State law time line.
	 2. Attorneys' Fees:
	   a. In addition to award of fees to parents, court may award fees to:
	     (1) Prevailing SEA or LEA against parents' attorney (a) who files complaint or other cause of action that is frivolous, unreasonable, or without foundation; or, (b) who continues to litigate after litigation clearly became frivolous, unreasonable, or without foundation.

Sec. 615(k).	***"Placement in Alternative Educational Setting."*** *Changes* and additions include: 1. Authority of School Personnel:

(continued)

TABLE 7.1 *(Continued)*

May consider unique circumstances on case-by-case basis when deciding whether to order change in placement for violation of student conduct code.

May remove child who *violates student conduct code* from current placement to IAES, another setting, or suspension for not more than 10 school days to the extent such alternatives are applied to child without disabilities.

Manifestation Determination:

(1) Except for short-term removals, within 10 school days of decision to change placement, LEA, parents, and relevant IEP team members (as determined by LEA and parents) shall review all relevant information (including IEP, teacher observations and relevant information provided by parents) to determine if:

    (a) the conduct was "caused by, or had a direct and substantial relationship to" child's disability; or,

    (b) the conduct was "direct result of LEA's failure to implement the IEP."

(2) If either instance above applies, the conduct is a manifestation of the disability, and the IEP team shall:

    (a) conduct a functional behavioral assessment, if not done prior to incident, and implement behavioral intervention plan or review previous plan for modification, as needed; and,

    (b) except when violations involve weapons, drugs, or serious bodily injury, return child to previous placement, unless parents and LEA agree to change in placement as part of modification of behavioral intervention plan.

2. Appeal:

    a. Either parent or LEA may request an appeal. SEA or LEA must arrange for expedited hearing, which must occur within 20 school days of date the hearing is requested and must result in a decision within 10 school days after hearing.

    b. During appeal, child remains in IAES pending decision or until expiration of time period allowed for students without

TABLE 7.1 *(Continued)*

	disabilities, whichever occurs first, unless parents and LEA agree otherwise.
	c. In reaching a decision, hearing officer may order a change in placement to (1) placement from which child was removed or (2) an IAES for not more than 45 school days if hearing officer determines that substantial likelihood in current placement of injury to child or others.
Sec. 616.	"Monitoring, Technical Assistance, and Enforcement."
	1. Federal and State Monitoring:
	a. Secretary shall (1) monitor implementation of law through oversight of general supervisory responsibility and the State performance plan (see below), and (2) require State to monitor LEAs.
	b. Primary focus of monitoring shall be on improving "educational results and functional outcomes for all children with disabilities."
	c. Monitoring priorities will be (1) provision of FAPE in least restrictive environment (LRE), (2) State's general supervisory authority, and (3) disproportionate representation of ethnic and racial minorities resulting in inappropriate identification.
Sec. 619.	*"Preschool Grants."* State reserve funds may be used for two new activities:
	1. Provision of Part C early intervention services to children eligible for preschool who previously received Part C services until they enter or are eligible for kindergarten; or,
	2. At a State's discretion, to continue service coordination or case management for families receiving services under Part C.
Sec. 635.	*"Requirements for Statewide System."* Additions to the system include:
	1. Services are based, *to the extent practicable, on scientifically based research* and available to infants/toddlers with disabilities, including *homeless children.*
	2. Child find includes "rigorous standards" of identification to reduce need for future services.

(continued)

TABLE 7.1 *(Continued)*

	3. Public awareness targets parents of premature infants or those with other physical risk factors associated with learning or developmental problems4 d. Training is provided for personnel in social and emotional development of young children.
National Center for Special Education Research	1. Title II establishes the National Center for Special Education Research 2. The Center will carry out research activities that are consistent with its mission to: a. Sponsor research to expand knowledge and understanding of the needs of infants, toddlers, and children with disabilities in order to improve developmental, educational, and transitional results.

Source: The Reauthorized Individuals with Disabilities Education Act 2004 (P.L. 108–446).

eight

The Teacher and School Liability

School districts, school officials, and teachers may incur liability for their tortious acts when these acts result in injury to students. A *tort* is an actionable or civil wrong committed against one person by another, independent of contract. If injury occurs based on the actions of school personnel, liability charges may be imminent. It may result from deliberate acts committed by another or acts involving negligence.

Students who are injured by school district personnel may claim monetary damages for their injury resulting from either intentional or unintentional torts. They also may, under certain conditions, seek injunctive relief to prevent the continuation of a harmful practice. Tort law further provides an opportunity for injured parties to bring charges when facts reveal that they received injury to their reputation.

In school settings, a tort may involve a class action suit affecting a number of school personnel, especially in cases involving negligent behavior. A tort may also involve actions brought against a single teacher, principal, or board member, depending on the circumstances surrounding the injury and the severity of the injury.

THE SCHOOL AS A SAFE PLACE

Schools are presumed to be safe places where teachers teach and students learn. The prevailing view held by the courts is that prudent professional educators, acting in place of parents, are supervising students under their care and ensuring, to the greatest extent possible, that they are safe. This doctrine is designed to provide parents with reasonable assurance that their children are safe while under the supervision of responsible professional adults.

This precept places an affirmative obligation on all certified school personnel to take necessary measures to ensure that the school environment is safe and conducive for students. In fact, teachers have been assigned three legal duties by the courts under *in loco parentis* (in place of parents)—to *instruct, supervise, and provide for the safety of students.* Although there is little expectation that students will never be injured, there is an expectation that school personnel will exercise proper care to ensure, to the greatest extent possible, that students are protected from harm.

When an unavoidable injury occurs, there is generally no liability. However, when injury is based on negligence, there are grounds for liability charges. Teachers, based on their legal duty, are expected to foresee that students may be injured under certain circumstances. Once determined, reasonable steps are necessary to prevent injury. In liability cases, courts will seek to determine if school personnel knew or should have known of an impending danger and whether appropriate steps were taken to protect students. Simply stated, there is no defense for failure to take reasonable steps to prevent foreseeable injury to students in school.

LIABILITY OF SCHOOL PERSONNEL

School personnel are responsible for their own tortious acts in the school environment. Liability involving school personnel normally falls into two categories: intentional torts and unintentional. *Intentional torts*—such as assault, battery, libel, slander, defamation (see Chapter 6 for a discussion of defamation), false arrest, malicious prosecution, and invasion of privacy—require proof of intent or willfulness; whereas simple negligence, as an *unintentional tort,* does not require such proof of intent or willfulness. In each case, liability charges may be sustained if the facts reveal that school personnel acted improperly or failed to act appropriately in situations involving students.

Individual Liability

In certain situations, school personnel may be held individually liable for their actions that result in injury to a student. Individual liability will not usually occur unless the plaintiff can demonstrate that a school employee's action violated a clearly established law and that the employee exhibited a reckless disregard for the rights of the plaintiff.[1]

The Supreme Court held in the *Davis* case that officials are shielded from liability for civil damages if their conduct does not violate clearly established statutory or constitutional rights of which a reasonable person would have known at the time of the incident.[2]

Vicarious Liability

Since school districts are deemed employers of teachers, they also may be held vicariously liable for the negligent behavior of their employees. Under the old theory of **respondeat superior**, the master is responsible only for authorized acts of its servants or agents. As applied in vicarious liability, the board rather than the principal is held liable for the tortious acts of its teachers, even though the board is not at fault. There is a requirement, under vicarious liability, that the teacher is acting within the scope of his or her assigned duties. This concept is most prevalent in cases involving negligence where class action suits are brought not only against the teacher but also the school district for alleged negligence by the teacher.

Foreseeability

Foreseeability is a crucial element in liability cases, especially in cases involving negligence. *Foreseeability* is defined as the teacher's or administrator's ability to predict or anticipate that a certain activity or situation may prove harmful to students. Once this determination is made, there is an expectation that prudent steps will be taken to prevent harm to students. Failure to act in a prudent manner may result in liability claims. For example, a teacher could be held negligent when he or she leaves the classroom for an extended period of time, and a student is injured during this absence. If the facts reveal that the students are immature, have a tendency to misbehave, and the teacher's absence is unauthorized, it is foreseeable that an injury might occur. Whether an injury is foreseeable or not is a question of fact that will be determined by a jury when deciding if liability should be imposed.

There are many instances when teachers and administrators are *expected to foresee* the potential danger associated with an activity or condition in the school. For example, if teachers or administrators observe broken glass panes in entry doors or in classrooms, it is foreseeable that a student, while entering the building or the room, might sustain an injury if contact is made with broken glass panes. In this instance, school teachers and administrators have an obligation to warn students of the impending danger and to exercise caution to ensure that students are not injured by making contact with this potentially dangerous condition. The broken panes should be reported to the proper authority and repaired promptly.

Similar expectations would occur in situations involving defective playground equipment, loose stair rails, or other *nuisances* (unsafe conditions) present in the school environment.

Nuisance

A *nuisance* may be described as any dangerous or hazardous condition that limits free use of property by the user. The existence of these conditions in schools may require school personnel to exercise extra care to ensure that students are protected from possible harm. The implication suggested here is that school districts have an obligation to maintain safe premises for students under their supervision. School district personnel have the responsibility to inform students of unsafe conditions and take steps to counsel students away from dangerous situations. Reasonable measures should be taken to remove or correct hazardous conditions as soon as they become known.

In some instances, the question of attractive nuisance arises. An *attractive nuisance* is a dangerous instrument or condition that has a special attraction to a less mature child who does not appreciate the potential danger and who could be harmed. The standard of care increases in attractive nuisance cases.

An attractive nuisance claim will be supported if the evidence suggests one or more of the following:

1. Those responsible for the property knew or should have known that children would be attracted to the hazardous condition.
2. The responsible party knew that the hazardous condition posed an unreasonable risk to children.
3. Children, because of their youth, were unaware of the risk.
4. The utility to the owner of maintaining the risk and the cost of eliminating it were slight, as compared to the risk to children.
5. The owner failed to exercise reasonable care in eliminating the risk.[3]

Negligence claims may be supported, however, if the evidence reveals that school personnel should have been aware of the hazard and were not diligent in responding to it. According to one court, however, it is unreasonable to expect that school personnel be required to discover or instantly correct every defect that is not of their own creation.[4] Reasonable action is required in cases involving nuisances. The courts have not required school personnel to ensure that premises are safe at all times. If reasonable measures, such as routine and periodic inspections and equipment repairs occur, unanticipated or unexplained accidents usually will not create liability charges against school personnel.

Because of their duty, teachers and administrators have a higher *standard of care* and are expected to *foresee* an accident more readily than would the average person. One of the fundamental questions raised by the courts in a case involving injury to a student is whether the teacher or administrator knew or should have known of the potential for harm to students. After an examination of facts, if the judge or jury determines that either should have known of the impending danger and failed to act appropriately, liability charges will likely be imposed.

INTENTIONAL TORTS

As mentioned earlier, torts fall into two categories: intentional and unintentional. An *intentional tort* results from a *deliberate act* committed against another person. It may or may not be accompanied by malice. When there is no intent to harm another person, but one proceeds intentionally in a manner that infringes on the rights of another, a tort has been committed. The law grants to each individual certain rights that must be respected by others. If by action or speech these rights are violated resulting in injury, a tort has been committed.

The most common forms of intentional torts affecting school personnel include *assault, battery, defamation, false imprisonment, and trespass to personal property.* (See a discussion of assault and battery in Chapter 4 and see a discussion of libel and slander in Chapter 6.)

Mental Distress

Mental distress is associated with liability. Charges of mental distress usually arise when someone exhibits conduct that exceeds the acceptable boundaries of decency. It is a form of tort liability that is construed to create mental distress in the absence of some type of physical injury. Historically, it has been difficult to prove mental distress in the absence of some type of physical injury. However, this situation has changed in recent years.

School personnel may be charged with mental distress if there is evidence that their behavior or conduct was calculated to cause serious emotional distress for students. School personnel typically are charged with inflicting mental distress when they use an unreasonable and unorthodox method of discipline designed to embarrass students or cause them to be ridiculed or humiliated in the presence of their peers.

As previously stated in Chapter 3, courts will allow school personnel to discipline students so long as the discipline is reasonable and consistent with school or district policy. There is a belief among many legal experts that actions by school personnel designed to embarrass students may be more damaging than physical harm. A student's self-esteem may be seriously damaged at a time when it should be growing and expanding. This is not intended to suggest that teachers or administrators cannot admonish a student in the classroom or hallway in front of his or her peers, but rather it serves as a caution to educators to exercise prudent judgment in doing so.

A teacher, however, may be held liable if the evidence reveals that there was an intentional act committed with the intent to humiliate or degrade when it is accompanied by proof of wantonness or malice.[5]

An illustration of what a teacher might face when poor judgment is exercised is found in an early 1973 case, *Celestine v. Lafayette Parish School Board,* in which a teacher was dismissed when it was determined that poor judgment and a lack of educational purpose resulted in the teacher requiring students to write a vulgar word 1,000 times in the presence of their classmates as a disciplinary measure for having uttered the word.[6] In many cases, students will rebel when they feel embarrassed by a teacher's or principal's action in the presence of their peers.

False Imprisonment

False imprisonment occurs when a student is detained illegally by a teacher or the principal. False imprisonment is considered to be an *intentional tort.* If a student is wrongfully detained for an unreasonable period of time for offensive behavior that does not warrant detention, a tort has occurred. If a student is confined by school personnel, there should be a reasonable basis for doing so and the confinement must be viewed as reasonable. School or district policy should serve as a guide in these situations.

Teachers and administrators may detain students and prevent their participation in playground activities, recess, and certain other extra school activities. They may detain students after school if the offense is clearly one that warrants detention and if parents are aware of the planned detention so that proper arrangements can be made to transport the student after the detention period has ended. Students should never be denied lunch breaks as a form of punishment. False imprisonment is not considered a major liability issue, but it is one that could prove difficult for school personnel if evidence reveals that detention was in violation of school or district policy and carried out with malice toward the student.

Trespassing on Personal Property

Trespassing on personal property is a tort that involves confiscating or interfering with the use of a student's personal property without proper authority. This is not an area that normally generates legal action, but it is one that school personnel should be mindful of since it most commonly involves teachers and administrators.

This intentional tort occurs frequently when school personnel confiscate various items from students during the school day. Many of these items may be in violation of school rules, may create disruption, or may cause harm to the student in possession of the item or to other students.

Teachers and administrators have the right to confiscate such items, but they do not have the right to keep them for an unreasonable period of time. If the item(s) is considered dangerous, the student's parent or guardian should be contacted and informed of the potential danger. Arrangements should be made with the parent or guardian to ensure that the item is not returned to the student.

UNINTENTIONAL TORTS

An *unintentional tort* is a wrong perpetrated by someone who fails to exercise that degree of care in doing what is otherwise permissible; in other words, the person acts negligently. Negligence is perhaps the most prevalent source of litigation involving injury to students. Many cases regarding negligence in school settings are class action in nature, implicating teachers, administrators, and boards of education. Defendants in these cases are usually released from the suit if facts reveal that they played no significant role in the injury.

Negligence is generally viewed as the failure to exercise a reasonable standard of care that results in harm or injury to another person. Most negligence cases involve civil wrongs, although there may be instances in which the accused faces both civil and criminal charges. In cases involving wanton negligence, such as injuries sustained by others based on violation of traffic laws, criminal charges may be appropriate, depending on the specific circumstances relating to the injury.

For example, when charges of negligence are sought by an injured student, certain requirements must be met. The student bringing the charges must be able to prove that four elements were present: standard of care, breach of duty, proximity or legal cause, and injury. Failure to establish each of the following elements invalidates charges of liability.

Standard of Care

The teacher or administrator owed a legal duty to protect the student by conforming to certain standards. Standard of care is an important concept in cases involving liability of school personnel. It requires that school personnel exercise the same degree of care that a person of *ordinary prudence* would exercise under the same or similar conditions. This standard of care will vary depending on particular circumstances. The level of care due to students changes based on the *age, maturity, experience,* and *mental capacity of students,* as well as the nature of the learning activities in which they are involved.

Breach of Duty

The teacher or administrator failed to meet these standards (duty of care). Breach of duty is determined in part based on the nature of the activity for which the educator is held responsible. Various school activities require different levels of supervision. The question normally posed by courts regarding breach is whether the conduct of school personnel met the standard of care required in a given situation. The second issue involves a determination as to whether school personnel should have foreseen possible injury and taken appropriate steps to prevent it.

Proximity or Legal Cause

The student must be able to demonstrate *proximate cause* (i.e., a causal relationship existed between the breach of duty and the actual injury sustained by the student). If a student is injured and the injury is not related to the teacher or administrator's failure to exercise the proper standard of care, there is no liability involved. *There must be evidence that links the injury directly to the failure of educators to act prudently in a given situation.*

Injury

The student must prove actual injury based on a breach of duty by the teacher or administrator. If there is no harm or injury suffered by a student, there is no liability. There must be evidence that actual injury did result either from acts committed by school personnel or their failure to act prudently in a given situation.

DEFENSES FOR NEGLIGENCE

Various defenses are used by school personnel to reduce or eliminate the impact of liability charges. These defenses are used, even in cases where the four elements of negligence (listed previously) are present.

Contributory Negligence

Contributory negligence is probably the most common defense employed against charges of negligence. When a teacher or administrator is charged with negligence, neither will be assessed monetary awards when contributory negligence is proven. However, there is a common law presumption regarding the incapacity of students to be contributorily negligent. Common law precedent suggests that a child under the age of 7 cannot be charged with contributory negligence. With children between the ages of 7 and 14, there is a reasonable assumption that they are incapable of contributory negligence. A child beyond the age of 14 may be assumed to be contributorily negligent, depending on the facts surrounding the injury. (These age limits are not absolute. They typically serve as guides in assessing whether contributory negligence did occur.)

Assumption of Risk

Assumption of risk is commonly used as a defense in situations involving various types of contact-related activities such as athletic teams, pep squads, and certain intramural activities. The theory supporting an assumption of risk is that students assume an element of risk to participate and benefit from the activity in which they wish to participate. Even though a student assumes an element of risk, it does not relieve school personnel in cases where they fail to meet a reasonable standard of care based on the age, maturity, risk, and nature of the risk associated with the activity.

Comparative Negligence

Comparative negligence, a relatively new concept, has grown in popularity in many states. It differs from contributory negligence in the sense that slight negligence by the plaintiff or injured party does not relieve the defendant or persons who may have greatly contributed to the injury.

Under comparative negligence, acts of those responsible are compared in the *degree of negligence* attributed in an injury situation. Juries will normally determine the degree of negligence, which may range from slight to ordinary to gross, depending on the circumstances. The jury will make a determination regarding the degree to which each party has contributed to an injury. If one party is found to have contributed more heavily to an injury than another, then that party will be assessed a greater proportion for damages. It does not prevent recovery by the injured party, but merely reduces the damages based on the fault of the injured persons.

Liability Costs

School personnel are well advised to affiliate with their state and national educational associations, since membership carries liability protection for its members during the execution of their professional duties. This obviously should not be the primary motivation for becoming affiliated, but should be considered as an important aspect of membership.

DUTIES OF SUPERVISION

All teachers and administrators are expected to provide reasonable supervision of students under their charge. The degree of supervision will vary with each situation. The less mature students are, the greater the need for supervision. The greater the potential for injury to students engaging in certain activities, the greater the need exists for supervision.

Whether school personnel have adequately fulfilled their duty of supervision is a question of fact for a jury to decide.

Each case rests on its merits. Courts will consider such factors as the nature of the activity involved, the age and number of students engaged in the activity, and the quality of supervision.

Supervision Before School and After School

School personnel have a responsibility to provide some form of supervision for students who arrive on campus before the normal school day begins. The amount of supervision depends on the circumstances involving early-arriving students. For example, foreseeability is established when a group of students arrives early or remains on campus after school without some form of supervision. Teachers and administrators are expected to foresee that students might be harmed if no form of supervision is provided. The same principle would apply for students who are retained on campus after school, waiting for their parents to arrive. Once foreseeability has been established, it is necessary to ensure that reasonable and prudent measures be taken.

There is no expectation that teachers and administrators guarantee that students will never be injured on school grounds. Certainly, this would be impossible to achieve. What must be demonstrated, however, is that reasonable measures were taken based on foreseeable harm to students. For example, there would be no expectation that teachers and administrators arrive or remain on campus during unreasonable hours to provide supervision. Although the courts have not addressed the time frame issue, per se, it would be a factor in deciding if teachers or administrators failed to meet a reasonable standard of supervision.

Certainly, parents should be informed in writing that school personnel are not available during the very early morning hours or later afternoon to supervise students. Parents should be discouraged from bringing their children to the campus during these early hours and be encouraged to pick them up promptly after school. Although these steps should be taken, they do not in themselves totally relieve teachers and administrators of supervisory responsibilities. The courts will usually reason that students are not present on campus due to their own choices. They are there because of parent decisions.

Administrators have the responsibility for assuring that the campus is safe for early-arriving students. Students and their parents should be informed of the behavior that is expected of students when arriving before or remaining after school. Once students are informed, some form of periodic supervision should occur to ensure that students are exhibiting proper conduct and are not engaged in potentially harmful activities.

Field Trips

School-sponsored field trips are considered to be mere extensions of normal school activities and thus require a reasonable standard of supervision by school personnel. In many instances, special supervision is required, due to the fact that students visit unfamiliar places and have a greater need for supervision. These activities generally provide valuable learning experiences for students. Because schools are moving toward connecting classroom learning to real-life situations, school-sponsored field trips will likely increase in popularity and instructional value.

Teachers are expected to exercise reasonable standards of supervision during field trip experiences. Students should be informed prior to the actual activities of the circumstances surrounding the activity. If there are special instructions or concerns, they should be properly conveyed by the teacher who has responsibility for supervising the field trip activity. Students, as well as parents, particularly those whose children are enrolled in the lower grades, should be informed of rules and expected behavior during the activity.

The *standard of care* involving field trips will vary depending on the age and maturity of students and the nature of the field experience. Teachers who organize field trips and administrators who approve them should be certain that there is adequate supervision in terms of *quality* and *quantity*. For example, it is foreseeable that if one teacher attempts to supervise 50 young, immature students during a trip to the zoo, some student might be harmed if an insufficient number of chaperones is unavailable to assist with supervisory duties.

It is an acceptable practice to request that parents serve as chaperones during these excursions, in which case parents should be fully informed of the nature of the activities involved, the type of students who will be supervised, and specific instructions regarding their supervisory duties. Students who are extremely active or have a history of misbehavior should be closely supervised by the classroom teacher, as it is foreseeable that they may be injured under certain conditions.

If field trips are well organized and supervised, they will meet the standard of care expected of school personnel while providing a valuable learning experience for students.

Parental Consent and Written Waivers

It is a common practice for school districts to require parents to sign permission slips allowing their children to participate in certain school-sponsored activities away from the school. This practice has obvious value, as parents are involved in the decision-making process regarding these activities.

In some cases, these consent forms also will contain a waiver or disclosure statement that relieves the school of any legal responsibility in the event a student is injured during a field-based, school-sponsored activity. Psychologically, this practice might discourage a parent who has endorsed such a form from raising a legal challenge in the event of an injury to his or her child, but it does not in any way relieve school personnel of their duty to provide reasonable supervision. *Such forms have very limited, if any, legal basis in law.* If a parent grants permission for the child to engage in an activity and also signs a waiver, legal action may still be brought against school personnel if negligence results in an injury to a student based on a lack of proper supervision. Teachers should be aware that permission forms, although valuable, do not abrogate their legal duty to supervise and provide for the safety of students during these excursions. Depending on the statute of limitations, it also is probable that a student may later bring suit against the district when he or she reaches majority age, even if the parent elects not to do so during the time in which the student actually received an injury.

GUIDES

School Liability

1. School district personnel must be aware of the standard of care that must be met in all activities as they instruct and supervise students in various activities to which they have been assigned.
2. Every teacher or administrator has a responsibility to ensure to the fullest extent possible that school buildings and grounds are safe for student use.
3. The absence of foreseeability by school personnel will not be upheld by the courts when the facts reveal that school personnel were expected to foresee the potential danger of a situation resulting in injury to a student.
4. Teachers have a legal duty to properly instruct, supervise, and provide a safe environment for students.
5. Reasonable and prudent decisions regarding student safety will withstand court scrutiny.

6. A higher standard of care may be expected of teachers during field trips and excursions involving students, especially in cases where students are viewed as licensees.

7. Students should not be coerced to use equipment or perform a physical activity for which they express serious apprehension. Coercion of this type could result in injury to the student and liability charges against school personnel.

8. Teachers and administrators should be reminded that the infliction of mental distress involving students may result in personal liability charges.

9. The conduct of school personnel should not be calculated to cause emotional harm to students.

10. When possible, teacher-student interactions that might tend to embarrass students or create mental distress should occur in private and not in the presence of their peers.

11. Board of education members may be held liable for their individual acts that result in the violation of a student's rights.

12. Students should not be detained after school for unreasonable periods of time for behavior that does not warrant detention.

13. Items retrieved from students, if not illegal, should be returned to students or their parents within a reasonable time frame and not retained permanently by school personnel.

14. A higher standard of care is necessary in laboratories, physical education classes, and contact sports.

15. School officials should provide some form of supervision for students before the school day begins or departing after the school day ends.

ENDNOTES

1. *Mitchell v. Forsyth,* 472 U.S. 511, 105 S.Ct. 2806 (1985).
2. *Davis v. Scherer,* 468, U.S. 183, 104 S.Ct. 3012 (1984).
3. Restatement of Torts, Second § 339.
4. *Jackson v. Cartwright School District,* 607 p. 2d 975 (Ariz. 1980).
5. *Gordon v. Oak Park School District No. 97,* 24 Ill. App. 3d 131, 320 N.E. 2d 389 (1974).
6. *Celestine v. Lafayette Parish School Board,* 284 So. 2d 650 (La. 1973).

nine

Discrimination in Employment

Constitutional, federal, and state statutes prohibit discriminatory practices in employment on the basis of sex, race, age, color, or religion. A significant number of federal statutes have been enacted specifically to address discrimination in employment. The social and political movements during the early 1960s focused major attention on the inequalities of employment opportunities and past discrimination practices. Many important pieces of federal legislation were enacted during the 1960s and 1970s, one of the most significant being Title VII of the Civil Rights Act of 1964, which prohibited employment discrimination based on race, color, religion, sex, or national origin.

The equal protection clause of the Fourteenth Amendment, which provides protection against group discrimination and unfair treatment, is used as a vehicle for individuals who seek relief from various forms of discrimination. A significant number of personnel practices in public schools pertaining to race, gender, age, and religion have been challenged, based on allegations of discrimination. Many school districts have responded to these challenges by noting that some of their current practices have been based on custom rather than a deliberate intent to discriminate. Nonetheless, courts have responded to challenges brought by school personnel in cases regarding alleged discrimination in employment practices based on issues involving gender, race, age, and pregnancy.

TITLE VII: DISCRIMINATION

One of the most extensive federal employment laws, the Civil Rights Act of 1964 Title VII, provides in part that

A. *It shall be an unlawful employment practice for any employee*
   1. *to fail or refuse to hire or to discharge any individual or otherwise to discriminate against any individual with respect to his compensation, terms and conditions or privileges of employment, because of such individual's race, color, religion, sex or national origin;*
   2. *to limit, segregate or classify his employees or applicants for employment in any way which would deprive or tend to deprive any individual of employment opportunities or otherwise adversely affect his status an employee, because of such individual's race, color, religion, sex or national origin.*
B. *It shall be an unlawful employment practice for an employment agency to fail or refuse to refer for employment, or otherwise to discriminate against any individual, because of his race, color, religion, sex or national origin, or to classify or refer for employment any individual on the basis of his race, color, religion, sex or national origin.*[1]

The original statute, enacted in 1964, covered employers and labor unions and did not apply to discriminatory employment practices in educational institutions until 1972, when the law was amended. Since its amendment, it has been utilized by educators to challenge questionable discriminatory practices in public schools. As stipulated in Title VII and Title IX, discrimination in employment based on gender is prohibited.

Title VII, which protects males and females from gender-based discrimination, was amended by the Civil Rights Act of 1991 (Public Law 102-166). This act provides for compensatory, punitive damages and a jury trial in cases involving intentional discrimination. An individual claiming discrimination under Title VII must file a complaint with the Equal Employment Opportunity Commission within 180 days following the alleged unlawful employment practice or within 300 days if the individual has filed a claim with a local or state civil rights agency. Failure to meet these time limits results in a loss of legal standing to challenge the alleged act. Remedies available under Title VII include compensatory damages, punitive damages, back pay, and reinstatement (for disparate treatment and incrimination), which will all be discussed later in this chapter.

To succeed under Title VII, a plaintiff must demonstrate that the employer's reason for the challenged employment decision is false and that the actual reason is discrimination.

This burden is oftentimes difficult to prove because there are very few instances in which plaintiffs have objective evidence or proof of discrimination. Many, however, have succeeded with indirect proof of discrimination in which the pretext for discrimination is established and the defendant is unable to convince the court that the reasons for his or her actions are worthy of belief.

Under the law of discrimination, for example, a teacher or administrator must demonstrate that he or she has made application for a position, is qualified for the position, and was not given fair consideration for the position. If the teacher or administrator is able to demonstrate a bona fide case of discrimination, then the burden shifts to the school district to demonstrate that its employment decision was not based on discriminatory practices.

In two historic noneducational cases, *McDonnell Douglas Corp. v. Green*[2] in 1973 and *Furnco Construction Corp. v. Waters*[3] in 1978, the Supreme Court developed a three-step procedure for Title VII challenges:

1. *The plaintiff carries the initial burden of establishing a prima facie case of employment discrimination.*
2. *The burden shifts to the defendant to refute the prima facie case by demonstrating that a legitimate nondiscriminatory purpose forms the basis for its actions.*
3. *If the defendant is successful in its contention, then the burden shifts back to the plaintiff to show that the defendant's actions were a mere pretext for discrimination. If, of course, the defendant can demonstrate the absence of a discriminatory motive, there is no need for step three.*[4]

Although these are noneducational cases, the same procedures apply in all cases involving alleged discrimination including those in public schools.

Sexual Discrimination

Discrimination based on sex is covered under Title IX of the Education Amendments Act of 1972, 20 U.S.C. § 1681 et seq., which prohibits sexual discrimination by public and private educational institutions receiving federal funds. The basic provision of the act states, "No person in the United States shall on the basis of sex, be excluded from participation in, be denied the benefits of, or be subjected to discrimination under any educational program or activity receiving federal financial assistance."[5]

Title IX is administered by the Office for Civil Rights (OCR) of the Department of Education. The provisions of this act are similar to the provisions in EEOC's guidelines found in Title VII. Title IX, also like Title VII, makes a provision for sexual distinctions in employment where sex is a bona fide occupational qualification.[6] Numerous challenges were raised during the mid-1970s by educational institutions questioning the applicability of Title IX to discrimination in employment issues. After a series of highly debated cases, the U.S. Supreme Court ruled in *Northaven Board of Education v. Bell* in 1988 that Title IX does apply to and prohibit sexual discrimination in employment.[7]

THE REHABILITATION ACT OF 1973 AND THE AMERICANS WITH DISABILITIES ACT OF 1990

The Americans with Disabilities Act (ADA), in conjunction with the IDEA, protects individuals with disabilities against discrimination and assures equal access and opportunity (see Chapter 7 on Individuals with Disabilities). Section 504 of the *Rehabilitation Act of 1973* prohibits discrimination against any otherwise qualified person who has a disability with respect to employment, training, compensation, promotion, fringe benefits, and terms and conditions of employment. The act states that "no otherwise qualified individual with handicaps . . . . shall solely by reason of his or her handicap be excluded from the participation in, be denied the benefits of, or be subjected to discrimination under any program or activity receiving federal financial assistance."[8] The ADA is similar to Section 504 and not only protects students with disabilities but any person who has a physical or mental impairment that substantially limits one or more major life activities, has a record of such impairment, or is regarded by others as having such an impairment.[9]

Major life activities, as interpreted by the ADA, may include such tasks as *caring for oneself, performing manual tasks, hearing, seeing, speaking, breathing, walking, learning and working.*[10] Section 504 extends beyond the school environment and covers all persons with disabilities in any program receiving federal financial assistance. Contrary to popular belief, the Rehabilitation Act does not require affirmative action on behalf of people with disabilities but rather equal opportunity.

The Americans with Disabilities Act prohibits the use of any standard criteria or administrative method that has the effect of discriminating or perpetuating discrimination based on a disability. The act states that no qualified person with a disability shall, by reason of such disability, be excluded from participation in or be denied the benefits of services, programs, or activities of a public nature or be subject to discrimination by any such public agency. School districts must make reasonable accommodations for persons with known disabilities, including job applicants and/or employees.

Qualifications for Employment

Any individual with a disability is qualified under ADA, if with or without reasonable accommodations, he or she can perform the core functions of the employment position held or desired to be held. Core job functions are not those that are considered marginal, but rather those that are essential to successfully execute designated tasks. The act prohibits any individual with a disability to be denied a job on the basis of not being able to meet physical or mental tasks that are not essential to effectively perform the desired job tasks. School boards must therefore make reasonable accommodations to any known physical or mental impairment of an otherwise qualified disabled individual. An employer may be exempt if it can be demonstrated that an undue hardship is involved in making a reasonable accommodation.

The term *undue hardship* means an action requiring significant difficulty or expense, when considered in light of the following factors:

1. *The nature and cost of the accommodation needed under this act*
2. *The overall financial resources of the facility or facilities involved in the provision of the reasonable accommodation; the number of persons employed at such facility; the effect on expenses and resources, or the impact otherwise of such accommodation upon the operation of the facility*
3. *The overall financial resources of the covered entity; and the overall size of the business of a covered entity with respect to the number of its employees, the number, type, and location of its facilities*
4. *The type of operation or operations of the covered entity, including the composition, structure, and functions of the work force of such entity; the geographic separateness, administrative, or fiscal relationship of the facility or facilities in question to the covered entity.*[11]

The burden of proof rests clearly with the employer.

Scope of Protection—Section 504 and ADA

Both ADA and the Rehabilitation Act impact public schools by prohibiting *disability-based discrimination*. When there is an allegation brought against school districts claiming discrimination, individuals bringing these charges may file a complaint with the Department of Education. If a violation is found, the Department of Education can mandate that federal funds be terminated, subject to judicial review of such action. Affected individuals also may seek relief in the courts for such violations. Available remedies may include injunctive relief and possible monetary damages when there is evidence of malicious intent or bad faith in discriminating against disabled individuals.

GUIDES

Americans with Disabilities

1. The Americans with Disabilities Act prohibits employment discrimination by employers with 15 or more employees.
2. School districts should develop nondiscriminatory policies regarding individuals with disabilities.
3. School districts should not segregate or limit job opportunities for individuals based on their disability.
4. School districts may not utilize and promote standards that have a discriminatory effect or perpetuate discrimination against persons with disabilities.
5. School officials may not deny employment to individuals with disabilities to avoid providing reasonable accommodations.
6. School districts must utilize standards that identify the skills of the person with disabilities rather than his or her impairments.
7. School districts should take appropriate measures to protect the confidentiality of medical records regarding individuals with disabilities.
8. School districts may be assessed compensatory and punitive damages for deliberate acts of discrimination against individuals who have disabilities.

Racial Discrimination

Court-ordered desegregation since the landmark 1954 *Brown v. Board of Education*[12] case has resulted in numerous challenges of racial discrimination, as predominantly black schools were closed and teachers and administrators were re-assigned to other schools. In many instances, blacks who held significant administrative positions prior to court-ordered desegregation found themselves in lesser positions or nonad-ministrative positions during the aftermath of the desegrega-tion movement. Even though the courts, in their ruling, attempted to achieve some degree of equity in assignment of blacks to predominantly white schools, their efforts fell short of achieving this objective.

The equal protection clause of the Fourteenth Amend-ment was relied on by blacks to eradicate patterns of racial discrimination in public schools. The equal protection stan-dards prohibited discrimination that can be linked with a racially motivated objective.[13] Unlike Title VII, no remedial action was attached to the equal protection clause, unless there was clear evidence that segregation was caused by de jure laws (official and deliberate laws or policies to promote segregation).

Title VII involves two basic types of claims: disparate treatment and disparate impact. The Supreme Court ad-dressed these two important issues in a later case involving discrimination on disparate treatment and disparate impact. *Disparate treatment* simply means that an employer treats some people more unfavorably than others regarding em-ployment, job promotion, or employment conditions based on race, color, religion, sex, or national origin. *Disparate im-pact* is merely a showing that numbers of people of a similar class are affected adversely by a particular employment prac-tice that appears neutral, such as a requirement that all em-ployees pass a test. The protected class categories usually involve race, gender, religion, and national origin. Disparate impact suits differ from disparate treatment in that they do not allege overt discriminatory action.

Religious Discrimination

The First Amendment and Title VII provide protection to em-ployees against religious discrimination. *Religion* is defined by Title VII to include all aspects of religious observances, prac-tices, and beliefs. Under this act, employers are expected to make reasonable accommodations to an employee's religious observance unless a hardship can be demonstrated. The bur-den of proof rests with the employer to demonstrate undue hardship. Most states have enacted legislation that requires employers to make accommodations for employees' religious practices. Thus, caution must be exercised by employers to ensure that the religious rights of employees are not violated. Employers also must be certain that the Establishment Clause of the First Amendment is not violated as well.

Age Discrimination

Age discrimination in public schools primarily affects teachers. In past years, many districts forced teachers to retire when they reached a specified age. These policies and practices were challenged by teachers under equal protection guarantees. Many of these challenges received mixed reviews by the courts. For example, the U.S. Supreme Court supported mandatory retirement for police officers, based on the rigorous physical demands associated with their positions. Conversely, the Seventh Circuit Court of Appeals rejected a practice of forced retirement for teachers at age 65, noting no justification to presume that teachers at age 65 lacked the academic skill, intellectual, or physical rigor to teach.[14]

All challenges and uncertainties became insignificant with the passage of the *Age Discrimination in Employment Act of 1967 (ADEA) as amended in 1978.* These acts effectively prohibited forced retirement of employees by protecting people above age 40 from discrimination on the basis of age with respect to hiring, dismissal, and other terms and conditions of employment. Prior to the act's amendment in 1978, the maximum age limit was set at 65 years. The 1978 amendment raised the limit to age 70. Amendments added in 1986 removed the limit *completely,* except for persons in certain public safety positions (e.g., police officers and fire fighters). The act covers teachers and other public employees. Many districts have instituted early retirement incentive plans. These are generally held acceptable by the courts, if they are strictly voluntary in nature. There can be no evidence suggesting that any *force* or *coercion* was used to enforce such plans. Currently, mandatory retirement plans for public schools, colleges, and universities are prohibited, as universities were exempt until 1993. They must now comply with the law.

PREGNANCY AND PUBLIC SCHOOL EMPLOYMENT

Teachers in public schools are protected by the Pregnancy Discrimination Act of 1978 (P.L. 95-555). This law is an amendment to Title VII, which extends protection to pregnant employees against any forms of discrimination based on pregnancy. The courts have been fairly consistent in their rulings regarding issues related to pregnancy. Prior to the enactment of this law, it was not uncommon for districts to enforce policy cut-off dates in which females were required to leave their positions due to their pregnant status. In a significant 1974 case, *Cleveland Board of Education v. LaFleur*,[15] the court held that mandatory maternity termination specifying the number of months before anticipated childbirth violated the equal protection clause of the Fourteenth Amendment, noting that arbitrary cut-off dates served no legitimate state interest in maintaining a continuous and orderly instructional program.

Districts may not assume that every teacher is physically unable to perform her teaching duties and responsibilities effectively because she is pregnant at a specific point in time. Courts have also not been supportive of district policies that barred a female teacher, after giving birth, from not returning to the district until the next regular semester or year. There have also been numerous challenges brought by female teachers regarding disability benefits, sick leave, and adequate insurance coverage.

Many of these challenges led to the enactment of the Pregnancy Discrimination Act of 1979. The basic intent of the act is to ensure that pregnant employees are treated in the same manner as other employees with respect to the ability to perform their duties. The act covers pregnancy, childbirth, and related medical conditions. Under this act, no longer can a woman be dismissed or denied a job or promotion due to pregnancy. Women must be able to take sick leave as other employees do for other illnesses and return to work when they are released by their physicians. Pregnancy must be treated as a temporary condition, thus entitling female employees to the same provisions of disability benefits, sick leave, and insurance coverage as any other employee who has a temporary disability.

FAMILY AND MEDICAL LEAVE ACT (FMLA)

The Family and Medical Leave Act was passed by Congress in 1993. It is designed to allow eligible employees up to a total of 12 work weeks of unpaid leave during any 12-month period for one or more of the following reasons:

1. For the birth and care of the newborn child of the employee
2. For placement with the employee of a son or daughter for adoption or foster care

3. To care for an immediate family member (spouse, child, or parent) with a serious health condition
4. To take medical leave when the employee is unable to work because of a serious health condition

Employers with 50 or more employees are covered by this act. An eligible employee is one who has been employed for at least 12 months or for at least 1,250 hours over the previous 12 months. The law permits the employee to choose to use accrued paid leave or the employer to require the employee to use accrued paid leave, such as vacation or sick leave for some or all of the FMLA leave period. When paid leave is substituted for unpaid FMLA leave, it may be counted against the 12 week FMLA leave entitlement, if the employer is properly notified of the designation when the leave begins.

An employer may raise questions of the employee to confirm whether the leave is needed or being taken qualifies for FMLA purposes. Periodic reports regarding the employee's status and intent to return to work after leave are permissible under the act. If an employer wishes to obtain another opinion, the affected employee may be required to secure additional medical certification at the employer's expense.

GUIDES

Discrimination

1. Punitive damages may be awarded in employment discrimination cases if the employer's conduct is viewed as egregious.
2. School districts will not be supported by the courts when there is evidence that their actions discriminated against employees on the basis of race, color, religion, gender, or national origin.
3. When *prima facie* evidence is presented by the employee, affected school officials must demonstrate that a compelling educational interest motivated their decisions.
4. School districts may not discriminate against employees because employees opposed practices made unlawful under discrimination laws or participated in an investigation regarding employment discrimination.
5. School officials may be held liable in any cases involving discrimination or harassment when it is determined that they were aware or should have been aware of these actions.
6. No employee may be coerced to retire from an employment position based on age nor may the employee be

     denied rights and privileges afforded other employees based on age, such as promotion and other benefits.

7. Race discrimination affects all employees, not merely minority employees.
8. Differential employment criteria may not be used that have an adverse affect on a special group of employees, even though these criteria may appear to be neutral.
9. Teachers and school personnel are entitled to rights under the Family and Medical Leave Act if they meet eligibility criteria.
10. It is unlawful for any employer to interfere with or restrain or deny the exercise of any right provided employees under the Family Medical Leave Act.

SEXUAL HARASSMENT

Sexual harassment is prohibited by Title VII and Title IX. In spite of these prohibitions, incidents of sexual harassment continue to grow at alarming rates. Cases involving charges of sexual harassment have increased rather dramatically in recent years. Based on statistics filed with the Equal Employment Opportunity Commission, sexual harassment charges more than doubled over a four-year period. Sexual harassment charges filed with EEOC declined by only 1 percent over this same period. These trends suggest that education and awareness training are critical factors in combating harassment in the workplace.

Interestingly, sexual harassment was not included in Title VII of the Civil Rights Act of 1964 until 1980. Its primary intent is to protect employees from harassment in their work environments. Harassment is considered to be a form of *sex discrimination.* It can manifest itself in many forms—verbal statements, gestures, overt behavior, and others.

The victim, as well as the harasser, may be a male or a female; he or she need not be of the opposite sex. The victim may not be the person harassed but may be anyone affected by the offensive conduct. Economic injury is not necessary to bring a successful case of harassment against a supervisor.

There are various levels of verbal harassment behavior, including, but not limited to, making personal inquiries of a sexual nature, offering sexual comments regarding a person's anatomy or clothing, and repeatedly requesting dates and refusing to accept "no" as an answer. Nonverbal harassment may include prolonged staring at another person, presenting personal gifts without cause, throwing kisses or licking one's lips, making various sexual gestures with one's hand, or posting sexually suggestive cartoons or pictures.

More serious levels may involve sexual coercion or unwanted physical relations. This type of behavior, *quid pro quo*, is commonly associated with superior-subordinate relationships in which the victim, for fear of reprisal, will unwillingly participate. This relationship is best described as a power relationship. In this case, the supervisor has the capacity to refuse to hire, promote, or grant or deny certain privileges, based on his or her position. In many instances, the promise of some job-related benefit is offered in exchange for sexual favors.

Another level of harassment involves *unwanted touching of another's hair, clothing, or body*. Undesirable acts involving hugging, kissing, stroking, patting, and massaging one's neck or shoulders are examples of physical harassment that contributes to a hostile work environment. Verbal harassment may include "off the cuff" comments, such as referring to females as "babe," "honey," or "sweetheart" or turning work discussions into sexual discussions including sexual jokes or stories.

Each of these levels represents a serious form of sexual discrimination for which the victim may recover damages. The burden rests with the victim to establish that the various levels of harassment are unwelcomed. Once established, the harasser has an obligation to discontinue such behavior immediately. Failure to do so usually creates a hostile work environment and results in charges of sexual harassment by the victim. Sexual harassment claims are sometimes difficult to pursue in court for the alleged victim. In many instances, embarrassing and graphic details must be revealed and are often denied by the person(s) against whom charges are made. Many victims of various forms of discrimination have been awarded monetary damages. The dollar amounts have increased significantly in recent years.

The definition of *harassment,* under the Civil Rights Act, is sufficiently broad to allow coverage for most forms of unacceptable behavior. Any type of sexual behavior or advance that is *unwanted* or *unwelcomed* is considered covered under the act. As indicated earlier, the person affected by such behavior has an obligation to inform the party that his or her behavior is *unwanted* or *unwelcomed*. It is difficult to claim harassment if the accused party is unaware that his or her behavior is unwelcomed. Although the regulation implementing sexual harassment is very broad, it is fairly prescriptive with respect to coverage. It defines sexual harassment in the following manner:

> *Unwelcome sexual advances, requests for sexual favors and other verbal or physical contact of a sexual nature constitute sexual harassment when (1) submission to such conduct is made either explicitly or implicitly a term or condition of an individual's employment (2) submission to or rejection of such conduct by an individual is used as the basis for employment decisions affecting such individuals or (3) such conduct has the purpose or effect of unreasonably interfering with an individual's work performance or creating an intimidating, hostile or offensive working environment.[16]*

Legally, employees may not be denied promotions or other benefits to which they are entitled on the basis of their unwillingness to accept sexual misconduct by their superiors, nor may they be subjected to hostile, unfriendly environments by superiors or peers if they too refuse to accept sexual misconduct. Under the act, every person is entitled to an environment free of unwelcome sexual conduct and one that allows the person to perform his or her duties without intimidation or fear of reprisal.

Guidelines established by the Equal Employment Opportunity Commission cover two types of sexual harassment previously mentioned: *quid pro quo* and *non-quid pro quo*. In *quid pro quo harassment*, an employee exchanges sexual favors for job benefits, promotion, or continued employment. In *non-quid pro quo* or a hostile environment, the employee is subjected to a sexually hostile and intimidating work environment that psychologically affects the employee's well-being and has an adverse affect on job performance.

A landmark case involving sexual harassment occurred in the private sector where a female bank employee filed action against the bank and her supervisor, alleging that she had been subjected to sexual harassment by her supervisor during her employment in violation of Title VII. The supervisor's contention was that the sexual relationship was consensual and had no bearing on the employee's continued employment. The bank indicated that it had no knowledge or notice of the allegation and therefore could not be held liable.

The Supreme Court, in a landmark ruling, *Meritor Savings Bank v. Vinson*,[17] in 1986, held that unwelcome sexual advances that create an offensive or hostile work environment violate Title VII. It further held that, although employers are not automatically liable for sexual harassment committed by their supervisors, absence of notice does not automatically insulate the employers from liability in such cases.

The significance of the ruling set the stage for subsequent sexual harassment cases by providing the definition of specific acts that fall within the category of harassment. The High Court suggested that Title VII guidelines are not limited to economic or tangible injuries. Harassment that leads to noneconomic injury may also violate Title VII. The Court considered the claim that sexual activity was voluntary to be without merit. The test, according to the Court, was whether such advances were unwelcomed.

Sexual harassment is prevalent in the United States and will likely continue to present legal challenges. This issue continues to evolve in the courts, where they are defining the legal limits of acceptable sex-related behavior in the workplace.

GUIDES

Sexual Harassment

1. District policies and procedures should be formulated to address sexual harassment for employees.
2. School officials should respond judiciously to any charges brought by employees regarding sexual harassment.
3. School officials should establish a zero tolerance policy so that everyone understands the school's position on issues involving harassment.
4. Staff development programs should be provided periodically to familiarize faculty and staff with all aspects of harassment and specific behavior considered to fall in the harassment category.
5. Faculty should be encouraged to report all violations through a well-defined, developed, and publicized grievance procedure.
6. School officials should create an environment in which school personnel feel comfortable in honestly reporting complaints of harassment free of any form of reprisal.
7. The confidentiality of those filing complaints should be protected to the greatest degree possible. Professional reputations can be damaged if charges prove to be false.

ENDNOTES

1. 42 U.S.C. § 2000e et seq.
2. *McDonnell Douglas Corp. v. Green,* 411 U.S. 792 (1973).

3. *Furnco Construction Corp. v. Waters,* 438 U.S. 567 (1978).
4. Ibid., 411, U.S. 792 (1973).
5. 20 U.S.C. § 1681 et seq. (1972).
6. 34 C.F.R. § 106.61.
7. *Northaven Board of Education v. Bell,* 456 U.S. 512 (1982).
8. 29 U.S.C. § 794 (A) (1988).
9. 29 U.S. C. § 706 (8) (B) (1988).
10. 34 C.F.R. § 104 3 (i) (2) (ii) (1991).
11. Ibid., (10).
12. *Brown v. Board of Education,* 347 U.S. 482, 74 S.Ct. 686 (1954).
13. *Adarand Constructors, Inc. v. Pena,* 63 U.S. 4523, 115 S.Ct. at 2111 (1995).
14. *Massachusetts Board of Regents v. Murgia,* 427 U.S. 307 (1976).
15. *Cleveland Board of Education v. LaFleur,* 414 U.S. 632 (1974).
16. 29 C.F.R. § 1604. 11 (a) (1991).
17. *Meritor Savings Bank v. Vinson,* 106 S.Ct. 2399 (1986).

ten

Teacher Freedoms

Public school teachers do not relinquish their personal rights as a condition to accepting an employment position in the public schools. Although teachers are expected to be sensitive to the professional nature of their positions and have a regard for the integrity of the profession, they do enjoy certain *constitutional freedoms* that must be respected by school authorities. Since teachers enter the profession with constitutional rights and freedoms, boards of education must establish a *compelling reason to restrict these freedoms.* In these instances, the burden rests with school officials to demonstrate that their actions are not *arbitrary, capricious, or motivated by personal and political objectives.*

The courts, in addressing conflicts involving constitutional freedoms of teachers, attempt to balance the public interest of the school district against the personal rights of each individual employee. Thus, teachers are subject to reasonable restraints only if a legitimate, defensible rationale is established by the school district.

SUBSTANTIVE AND PROCEDURAL CONSIDERATIONS

As stated in Chapter 3, there are two types of due process, both of which apply to teachers: procedural and substantive. *Procedural due process* means that when a teacher is deprived of life, liberty, or property, a prescribed constitutional procedure must be followed. Briefly stated, the teacher deprived must be given proper notice that he or she is to be deprived of life, liberty, or property. The teacher must be provided an opportunity to be heard and the hearing must be conducted in a fair manner. Failure to follow procedural requirements will result in a violation of the teacher's constitutional rights. *Substantive due process* means that the state must have a valid objective when it intends to deprive a teacher of life, liberty, or property, and the means used must be reasonably calculated to achieve its objective.

Most important, both procedural and substantive requirements must be met in teacher dismissal proceedings. Many administrative decisions that were correct in substance have been overturned on appeal to higher authority based simply on the grounds that procedural requirements were not met. Conversely, procedural requirements may have been met by school officials when the evidence revealed that a valid reason did not exist that warranted depriving a teacher of his or her substantive rights. The administrative decision in this case would be overturned as well.

FREEDOM OF EXPRESSION

By virtue of the First Amendment to the Constitution, teachers are afforded rights to freedom of expression. Within limits, they enjoy the same rights and privileges regarding speech and expression as other citizens. Free speech by teachers, however, is limited to the requirement that such speech does not create *material disruption* to the educational interest of the school district. Material disruption, for example, may involve an interference with the rights of others or may involve speech that creates a negative impact on proper school discipline and decorum. The level of protection provided teachers is generally lower in cases where the teacher speaks on matters that are personal in nature, as opposed to those that are of interest to the community.

In either case, school officials may not justifiably prohibit or penalize the teacher in any manner for exercising a constitutionally protected right without showing that a legitimate state interest is affected by the teacher's speech or expression. As usual, in cases where the teacher's speech is restricted, the burden of proof justifying such restriction rests with school officials. Districts have succeeded in their actions to restrict speech and to discipline teachers when there was evidence that the teacher's personal speech undermined authority and adversely affected working relationships or rendered the teacher unfit to teach. In the absence of such showing, the teacher's speech is protected.

In fact, the Supreme Court addressed the application of the First Amendment in employment situations by emphasizing in the *Connick v. Myers* case the distinction between speech involving public concern and grievances regarding internal personnel matters. Expressions regarding public concerns, according to the High Court, receive First Amendment protections, whereas ordinary employee grievances are to be handled by the appropriate administrative body without involvement of the Court.[1] In this case, the issue involved a petition that was circulated within an office related to the proper functioning of the office. This type of personal speech did not receive First Amendment protection.

Speech Outside the School Environment

Teachers are afforded First Amendment rights outside the school environment. They may speak on issues that are of a personal interest, even though their speech may not be deemed popular by school district officials. When exercising such speech, however, *teachers should preface their comments by indicating that they speak as a private citizen rather than as employees of the board.* This public disclosure is significant in establishing that a teacher's speech not be viewed as the official position of the school district. This disclosure further reinforces the notion that the teacher possesses the same First Amendment privileges as regular citizens. Although teachers enjoy First Amendment rights, those rights are not without reasonable restrictions based on the nature of the position held and the positive image teachers are expected to project with students and the community. In all cases, the teacher's speech should be professional in nature and not designed to harm or injure another's reputation or render the teacher unfit, based on the content of the speech itself. These standards apply whether the speech is verbal or written.

A Connecticut court generated the following guidelines involving freedom of expression issues regarding the operation of the public schools:

1. *The impact on harmony, personal loyalty and confidence among co-workers*
2. *The degree of falsity of statements*
3. *The place where speech or distribution of material occurred*
4. *The impact of the staff and students, and*
5. *The degree to which the teacher's conduct lacked professionalism.[2]*

Generally, a teacher's freedom of expression rights are protected. They are, however, subject to reasonable considerations regarding order, loyalty, professionalism, and overall impact on the operation of the school.

Academic Freedom

Public school teachers are afforded a degree of academic freedom in their classrooms, based on the teacher's right to teach and the students' right to learn. Academic freedom, as a concept, originated in the German universities during the nineteenth century with the expressed purpose of allowing professors to teach any subject they deemed educationally appropriate.

Public school teachers, of course, are not provided broad latitude that allows them to introduce any subject into their teaching. *Academic freedom is a limited concept in public schools.* It supports the belief that the classroom should be a marketplace of ideas and that teachers should be provided freedom of inquiry, research, and discussion of various ideas and issues. Since public school teachers teach children of tender years who are impressionable, their freedom of expression in the classroom will be affected by factors such as grade level, age, and the experience and readiness of students to handle the content under discussion and the appropriateness of the content.

Teachers should also be certain that the subject matter introduced into classroom discussion is within the scope of students' intellectual and social maturity levels. *A public school teacher is further restrained by the requirement that content introduced into classroom discussion be related to and consistent with the teacher's certification and teaching assignment.* Controversial material that is unrelated to the subject taught and inappropriate, based on content, will not be supported by the courts.

FREEDOM OF ASSOCIATION

The First Amendment guarantees citizens the right to peacefully assemble. Freedom of association is included within this right of assembly since teachers as citizens are entitled to the same rights and privileges provided other citizens. *Freedom of association grants people the right to associate with other persons of their choice without threat of punishment.* Although teachers enjoy these rights, they should exercise them in light of the nature and importance of their positions as public employees. Further, they should be concerned with the "role-model image" they project and the impact of their actions on impressionable young children. The Supreme Court of Iowa stated, "A teacher's conduct involving shoplifting impacted her ability to be an effective role model for students."[3]

In some instances, teachers who had been involved in organized labor organizations or educational associations received questionable treatment by their school districts. This treatment was oftentimes reflected in the form of demotions, unwarranted transfers, nonrenewals, and even terminations. The courts will no longer support this type of treatment of teachers.

Since the late 1960s, there has been a discernible trend by the court toward providing teachers more freedom regarding their personal lives than was true in the past. Courts now hold that teachers, including administrators, are free to join their professional organizations, assume a leadership role, campaign for membership, and negotiate with the school board on behalf of the organization without fear of reprisal. School personnel must ensure that their participation in external organizations does not, in any manner, reduce their effectiveness as district employees or create material or substantial disruption to the operation of the district.

School personnel may also engage in various types of political activities. They may become a candidate for public office or campaign for their favorite candidate. However, school personnel may be requested to take personal leave when they run for public office. These are permissible activities, so long as these occur after school hours and do not interfere with job effectiveness.

POLITICAL RIGHTS

Based on the State Interest Test, state laws prohibiting public employees from participating in all types of political activities have been deemed unconstitutional. Public school teachers have the same political rights and freedoms enjoyed by all citizens. These include, but are not limited to, running for public office, campaigning for themselves or others, developing and expounding political ideologies, and engaging in political debate. These rights, however, should be exercised with a degree of restraint inasmuch as they are not unlimited. There has to be at all times an awareness on the teacher's part of the effect of his or her actions on others, especially children. Teachers should also ensure that engaging in political classroom performance is not adversely affected based on political activity. Teachers must limit their political activity to acts away from the classroom and outside of the normal school day. They must further ensure that their political activity in no way interferes with or infringes on their duties and responsibilities in the classroom.

In fact, there seems to be a trend toward greater political freedom for teachers by the courts so long as the teacher exhibits prudent professional behavior, does not neglect his or her professional duties, and does not use the classroom as a political forum.

DRESS AND GROOMING

Numerous cases regarding personal appearance issues involving teachers have been litigated by the courts. School authorities generally contend that proper dress and decorum create a professional image of teachers that impact positively on students. Teachers, on the other hand, contend that dress code regulations governing their appearance invade their rights to free expression. Teachers further believe that they should enjoy freedom without undue restrictions on their personal appearance.

The courts generally have not been in disagreement regarding the authority of school officials to regulate teacher appearance that may disrupt the educational process. What has not been settled, however, is the *degree of constitutional protection teachers are entitled to receive in disputes regarding dress and the type of evidence needed to invalidate restrictions on dress.* To further complicate the issue, community standards and mores are also factors considered in dress and grooming rulings. School districts have traditionally restricted dress that is contrary to acceptable community norms. The courts have also established the position that school dress codes must be reasonably related to a legitimate educational purpose, which must be justified by standards of reasonableness.

Rules that restricted dress based on health, safety, material and substantial disruption, or community values have been generally supported by the courts. Rules that extended beyond these areas generally have not been supported. It seems evident that the courts recognize that teachers should be free of unreasonable restrictions governing their appearance. However, the difficulty comes with variations in standards by different communities, as well as changing societal norms.

The courts will not support restrictive dress and grooming codes that are unrelated to the state's interest. When challenged, the district must demonstrate that the code is related to a *legitimate educational purpose,* and not designed to place undue and unnecessary restrictions on teachers' dress. The burden of proof rests with the school district.

UNWED PREGNANT TEACHERS

Courts tend to vary in rulings regarding unwed pregnant teachers. During the early 1960s and 1970s, courts were more inclined to rule against single teachers who were dismissed by school boards when they reported their pregnancy. However, during the mid-1970s and early 1980s, with increased attention focused on individual rights of teachers, courts became less inclined to rule against unwed pregnant teachers without carefully weighing all aspects of each case. In doing so, the courts considered the teacher's overall performance record, the impact of the teacher's actions on students, and, more important, the extent to which the teacher's actions adversely affects her effectiveness as a teacher. Courts may also consider community standards and the degree to which the teacher's conduct violates the ethics of the community and renders the teacher unsuitable to teach.

RIGHT TO PRIVACY

It is commonly held that teachers enjoy a measure of privacy in their personal lives. These rights should be respected to the extent that they do not violate the *integrity* of the community or render the teacher ineffective in performing professional duties. Within the context of privacy rights, teachers may exercise personal choices, ranging from living with a person of the opposite sex to other lifestyle choices. In many instances, school boards cite privacy issues involving teachers as the basis to dismiss them from their employment positions or recommend revocation of the teaching certificate. Although there does not appear to be a clear distinction drawn between protected and unprotected lifestyle choices, the burden of proof resides with school officials to demonstrate that lifestyle choice adversely affects the integrity of the district or that the teacher's conduct has a detrimental affect on his or her relations with students.

In exercising lifestyle choices, teachers must also be reminded of the professional nature of their position and the impact that their behavior has on children who often view them as role models. For example, when a teacher engages in a private adulterous activity, it does not necessarily follow that this act, within itself, forms grounds for action to be taken against the teacher. Teachers are entitled to rights to privacy, as are other citizens, and these rights must be respected. Whether a school district is successful in penalizing a teacher for private conduct would again be based on a district's capacity to demonstrate that the teacher's effectiveness is impaired by his or her conduct. The burden of proof clearly resides with school officials.

When a teacher has demonstrated a strong record of teaching, has been effective in relationships with students, and is respected in the community by his or her peers, it is unlikely that school officials will succeed in bringing serious actions against the teacher, such as removal from an employment position or revocation of certificate. On the other hand, if private conduct becomes highly publicized to the point that the teacher's reputation and relationships with parents and students have been impaired, rendering the teacher ineffective in executing his or her duties, appropriate actions may be taken by school officials and supported by the courts.

In a significant 1986 ruling, the U.S. Supreme Court in *Bowers v. Hardwick* held that consenting adults did not have a fundamental right to engage in homosexual activity.[4] Consequently, school boards may dismiss teachers for engaging in homosexual acts, particularly in cases where these acts are prohibited by criminal law. In such case, there should be a connection between engaging in a homosexual act and overall fitness to teach.

GUIDES

Teacher Freedoms

1. Teachers do not lose their constitutional rights when they enter the educational profession. Within reasonable limits, they possess the same constitutional rights as do other citizens.
2. Teachers should avoid personal attacks or libelous or slanderous statements when exercising freedom of expression rights or expressing concerns of interest to the community.
3. Teachers should not knowingly report false information when criticizing the district's decision or actions.
4. School officials may not penalize or otherwise discriminate against teachers for the proper execution of their First Amendment rights, especially regarding issues of public concern.
5. Academic freedom is a limited concept. Teachers should introduce appropriate material in the classroom that is

related to their assigned subject matter. The classroom should never be used as a forum to advance the teacher's political or religious views.

6. Teachers may associate with whomever they wish, so long as their association does not involve illegal activity or their behavior renders them unfit to perform their job functions effectively.

7. Dress, grooming, and appearance may be regulated by school boards if a compelling educational interest is demonstrated or if such codes are supported by community standards.

8. Teachers are entitled to rights of privacy and cannot be legally penalized for private noncriminal acts that have no impact on teacher effectiveness.

RELIGIOUS FREEDOMS

The First Amendment guarantees religious freedoms to all citizens. Title VII of the Civil Rights Act of 1964 further prohibits any forms of discrimination based on religion. Therefore, it is unlawful for a school district to deny employment or to dismiss or fail to renew a teacher's contract based on religious grounds. Teachers, like all citizens, possess religious rights that must be respected. As with all rights, religious rights are not without limits. Since teachers are public employees and schools must remain neutral in all matters regarding religion, there are reasonable restraints that impact the exercise of religious rights in the school setting. However, teachers are completely free to fully exercise their religious rights outside of normal school activities.

For example, teachers may not refuse to teach certain aspects of the state-approved curriculum based on religious objections or beliefs. The courts recognize the existence of a teacher's religious rights, but they also recognize the compelling state interest in educating all children. Courts generally hold that education cannot be left to individual teachers to teach the way they please. An elementary teacher was not supported by the Sixth Circuit Court when she required students to view a videotape of her singing a religious song.[5] Teachers have no constitutional right to require others to submit to their views and to forego a portion of their education they would otherwise be entitled to enjoy. In short, teachers cannot subject others, particularly students, to their religious beliefs or ideologies. They, too, must remain neutral in their relationship with students.

Use of Religious Garb by School Personnel

The wearing of religious garb by public school teachers has created legal questions regarding freedom of expression rights versus religious violations based on dress. It has been well established that public school districts may not legally deny employment opportunities to teachers based on their religious beliefs or affiliation. However, the wearing of religious garb by public school teachers raises the issue as to whether such dress creates a sectarian influence in the classroom. Many state statutes prohibit public teachers from wearing religious garb in the classroom. Some legal experts believe that the mere presence of religious dress serves as a constant reminder of a teacher's religious orientation and could have a proselytizing affect on children, since they are impressionable, particularly in the lower grades.

In contrast, public school teachers advance the argument that religious dress is a protected right regarding freedom of expression. The courts, however, have clearly established the position that the exercise of one person's rights may not infringe on the rights of others and that public interest supersedes individual interests. Further, prohibiting a teacher from wearing religious dress does not adversely affect the teacher's belief. It merely means that teachers cannot exercise their beliefs through dress during the period of the day in which they are employed. There is no interference outside of the school day. Thus, a teacher is free to fully exercise religious rights and freedoms outside normal hours of employment. The courts have not reached total consensus on this issue.

TITLE VII: RELIGIOUS DISCRIMINATION

Title VII addresses any forms of religious discrimination regarding employment. *Religion* is defined under Title VII to include "all aspects of religious observances, practices and beliefs."[6] This section also requires that an employer, including a school board, make reasonable accommodations to the employee's religion, unless the employer can demonstrate the inability to do so based on undue hardship. Furthermore, school officials must respect and, when possible, make allowances for teachers' religious observances if such observances do not create substantial disruption to the educational process. Accommodations may include personal leave to attend a religious convention or to observe a religious holiday. Unless there is a showing of undue hardship, reasonable accommodation must be provided. If such requests are deemed excessive, resulting in considerable disruption to children's education, a denial would be appropriate.

In cases where school officials deny excessive leaves for religious purposes, the burden of proof rests with the teacher to demonstrate that the officials' decision involved the denial of certain religious freedoms. If the teacher is able to demonstrate discriminatory intent, then the burden shifts to school officials to show a legitimate state interest, such as a disruption of educational services to children. The Equal Education Opportunity Commission (EEOC) or a court would be hard pressed to challenge a legitimate state interest involving the proper education of children.

GUIDES

Religious Discrimination

1. The religious rights of teachers must be respected, so long as they do not violate the establishment clause of the First Amendment by creating excessive entanglement in the school.
2. School officials must make reasonable accommodations for teachers regarding observance of special religious holidays, so long as such accommodations are not deemed excessive or disruptive to the educational process.
3. Teachers should not be coerced to participate in nonacademic ceremonies or activities that violate their religious beliefs or convictions.
4. Teachers may be requested to present documentable evidence that a religious belief or right is violated in cases involving the performance of their nonacademic duties.
5. No form of religious discrimination may be used to influence decisions regarding employment, promotion, salary increments, transfers, demotions, or dismissals.

ENDNOTES

1. *Connick v. Myers,* 461, U.S. 138 (1983).
2. *Gilbertson v. McAlister,* 403, F.Supp. 1 (D. Conn. 1975).
3. *Board of Directors of Lawton-Bronson v. Davies,* 489 N.W. 2d 19 S.Ct. of Iowa, 1992.
4. *Bowers v. Hardwick,* 478 U.S. 186 (1986).
5. *De Nooyer v. Livonia Public Schools,* 12 F 3d 211 (6th Circuit 1993), Cert. denied 114 S.Ct. 1540 (1994).
6. 42 U.S.C. § 2000e (2).

eleven

Tenure, Dismissal, and Collective Bargaining

TENURE

Tenure in public schools is prescribed by state statute. Although there are variations among states, tenure laws are designed to protect good teachers. The *tenure contract* is designed primarily to provide a measure of security for teachers and to ensure that they are protected from arbitrary and capricious treatment by school officials. Tenure also is viewed as a means of providing a degree of permanency in the teaching force from which students ultimately benefit. Any teacher who earns tenure or continuing service status also acquires a property right or a legitimate claim to the teaching position. Once a property right is acquired, the teacher may be dismissed only for cause. Tenure does *not* guarantee continued employment, but it does ensure that certified school personnel may not be arbitrarily removed from their employment positions without due process of law. The intended purpose of tenure laws has been described by the courts. One court described it in this manner:

> *While tenure provisions . . . protect teachers in their positions from political or arbitrary interference, they are not intended to preclude dismissal where the conduct is detrimental to the efficient operation and administration of the schools of the district. . . . Its objective is to improve the school system by assuring teachers of experience and ability a continuous service based upon merit, and by protecting them against dismissal for reasons that are political, partisan or capricious.[1]*

149

Through this protection, teachers are insulated from special interest groups and political factions, thereby enabling them to perform their professional duties without undue interference. When this occurs, the educational system is improved and the students derive the benefits of quality education.

Acquisition of Tenure

In a number of states, tenure may be attained only after the teacher has successfully completed three successive years in the same district during the probationary period and receives an offer for reemployment for the succeeding year. The *probationary period* is one in which the nontenured teacher is seeking tenure. School boards are provided broad latitude in determining whether tenure should be granted. During the probationary period, a teacher may be *nonrenewed at the end of the contract year without cause or dismissed during the contract year with cause.* In the case of the latter, the teacher must be afforded full due process rights. There is no requirement for due process provisions in cases involving nonrenewal, unless the teacher is able to demonstrate that nonrenewal was based purely on personal or political motives, or was motivated by arbitrary and capricious actions involving infringement on constitutional rights. This is usually a difficult burden of proof to meet, but the ultimate burden rests with the probationary teacher.

Since state laws prescribe that certain substantive and procedural requirements be met regarding tenure, it is essential that school districts adhere to these requirements (see Chapter 9 for discussion of substantive and procedural issues). Generally, state statutes identify a specific date in which a probationary teacher must be informed that employment opportunities will no longer be available for the succeeding year. In most states, no reasons need be given for nonrenewal of a probationary teacher's contract. This notice informing the teacher of nonrenewal is normally forwarded to the teacher by certified or registered mail to the latest known address on or before a specified date. If the district fails to meet this requirement, the teacher may have gained employment for the following year. When a teacher has completed three consecutive years in the same district and did not receive timely notice of nonrenewal, the teacher may have acquired tenure by *default.*

In sum, nontenured status involves

- No expectation for employment beyond the contracted year

- No right to be provided reasons for nonrenewal
- No right to due process
- No hearing

These conditions are valid unless the nontenured teacher produces evidence that a liberty or property right exists, in which case due process must be provided. A *liberty right* exists when damaging statements are communicated that may limit the teacher's range of future employment opportunities. A *property right* exists only if the nontenured teacher's contract is canceled during the contract or school year.

Nonrenewal

The primary reason due process does not apply to probationary status centers on a limited property interest. During the probationary period, the teacher typically is offered a one-year contract that is renewable each year, if the school board elects to do so. The probationary teacher then has a property right only for the duration of the one-year contract. When the contract period ends each year, the teacher loses the inherent property right because both the teacher and the district have met contractual obligations to each other. Due process and cause are necessary only if there is a showing that a property interest continues to exist. A property interest does not exist if there is no legal contract in force. As stated previously, if a district decides to dismiss a probationary teacher during the contract period, then full due process provisions are required, including notice, cause, and a formal hearing, because the teacher has a property right for the contract year.

GUIDES

Tenure

1. Teachers are entitled to fundamental fairness, irrespective of tenure status.
2. Tenure is not designed to protect teachers who are inept or ineffective but rather those who are competent and effective.
3. Tenured teachers may be dismissed only for specified reasons that are based on objective and documentable evidence.
4. Due process procedural safeguards, as established by state statutes, should be followed to ensure that dismissal decisions are legally defensible.

5. Nonrenewal of a nontenured teacher's contract does not generally require due process or reasons, unless there is an alleged constitutional violation or a liberty or property right involved.

Teacher Evaluation

The primary purpose of teacher evaluation is to assess a teacher's effectiveness and to provide guidance and direction for improvement. Most school districts have well-developed policies and procedures along with prescribed evaluation forms that guide the evaluation process. Ideally, the teacher should be informed of a proposed evaluation. Evaluations should be administered systematically. The teacher's performance should be documented, including strengths and areas in need of improvement. To the greatest degree possible, documentation should be quantified. Evaluation scores should be compared with predeterminant standards to determine teacher effectiveness.

Ideally, teacher effectiveness should be a measure of student learning outcomes. A thorough improvement plan should be developed based on evaluation results with a reasonable time frame given to the teacher to meet expected performance standards. Administrative assistance and support should be provided during the time period in which the teacher is expected to meet expected performance standards. If evaluations are used for any purpose other than the improvement of performance, the teacher should be informed of their use.

There should be provisions for the teacher to rebut any evaluation thought to be unfair. The teacher should also have an opportunity to seek another evaluation by an alternate supervisor if the teacher believes that the previous evaluation was inaccurate or extraordinarily subjective. Fundamental fairness should guide the evaluation process. Courts are generally reluctant to substitute their judgment in cases involving teacher evaluation. However, they will address issues involving procedural matters with respect to fundamental fairness.

GUIDES

Teacher Evaluation

1. Evaluation criteria should be communicated to teachers and applied fairly and consistently.

2. If evaluations are used for any purpose other than improvement of performance, the teacher should be informed of their use.
3. Administrative support is an essential component of the Teacher Performance Improvement Plan.

DISMISSAL FOR CAUSE

Dismissing a teacher for cause is a serious matter, since the teacher has an inherent property right to hold the employment position. State statutes prescribe permissible grounds on which dismissal is based. In these cases, the burden of proof resides with the board of education to show cause based on a preponderance of evidence. The obvious benefit of tenure is that dismissal cannot occur without a formal hearing and the presentation of sufficient evidence to meet statutory requirements. This assures the teacher that procedural and substantive due process requirements are met.

Tenure laws include grounds for dismissal in virtually all states. Although there are variations among states, these grounds normally include *incompetency, insubordination, neglect of duty, immorality, justifiable decrease in the number of teaching positions,* or *financial exigency,* and a statement indicating "*other good and just cause.*" This latter phrase provides the board with broader latitude to address other grounds that may not be specified by statute. A board of education may dismiss a teacher for almost any reason, so long as the reason is valid and meets the procedural due process requirements.

Incompetency

One of the more frequently used grounds for dismissal involves charges of incompetency. *Incompetency* is a vague term in many respects. In some states, incompetency is used as the sole grounds for dismissal, using almost any reason to comprise this category. Most commonly, *incompetency* refers to inefficiency, a lack of skill, inadequate knowledge of subject matter, inability or unwillingness to teach the curriculum, failure to work effectively with colleagues and parents, failure to maintain discipline, mismanagement of the classroom, and attitudinal deficiencies. Since the court views the teaching certificate as *prima facie* proof of competency, the burden of proof challenging a teacher's competency rests with the school board. The competent teacher is generally viewed as a person who has the knowledge, skills, and intelligence of the average or ordinary teacher.

If charges of incompetency are brought against a teacher, these charges should be preceded by systematic evaluations and documentation of performance as well as a thoroughly developed Teacher Performance Improvement Plan. Proper documentation and a reasonable time frame designed to allow the teacher to meet expected performance standards are critical to sustain charges of incompetence should it become necessary to do so.

Insubordination

Insubordination is generally viewed as the willful failure or inability to obey a reasonable and valid administrative directive. In most cases, there is a discernible pattern in the teacher's behavior that reveals he or she has been insubordinate. However, there are other instances in which one serious violation may form the basis for charges of insubordination. Most cases involving insubordination are those in which the teacher has been given distinct warning regarding the undesirable conduct and has failed to heed the warning. In such cases, charges of insubordination are usually sustained.

To succeed with insubordination charges, there must be documented evidence of the alleged misconduct with further evidence that the administrative order or directive was valid. Insubordination charges are more likely to succeed when they are linked with teaching performance or related academic issues. If the evidence reveals that the directive or administrative order was biased against the teacher or unreasonable, insubordination charges will be difficult to defend. Also, there should be no evidence that the order or rules violated the teacher's personal rights.

Neglect of Duty

Neglect of duty occurs when a teacher fails to execute assigned duties. Neglect may be intentional or unintentional based on ineffective performance. One court defined *neglect of duty* as the failure to carry out professional obligations and responsibilities in connection with classroom or other school-sponsored activities.[2] Another court held that neglect of duty involving performance is not measured against a standard of perfection but must be measured against the standard required of others performing the same or similar duties.[3]

Immorality

Immorality is cited in relevant state statutes as grounds for dismissal and involves conduct that violates the ethics of a particular community. Some state laws refer to immorality as "unfitness to teach" or behavior that sets a poor example for students and violates moral integrity. One court has held that the conduct in question must not only be immoral under the particular community standards test but must also be found to impair the teacher's ability to teach.[4] This latter statement seems to reflect the consensus of court decisions regarding issues of immorality in that there must be a showing that the conduct in question impairs the teacher's effectiveness in the classroom.

Conduct Involving Morality

Public school teachers serve in highly visible and significant positions. In many instances, they exert important influence on the views of students and the formation of their values. Based on their roles, there is an expectation that a teacher's character and personal conduct be elevated above the conduct of the average citizen who does not interact with children on a daily basis.

One of the most quoted definitions of the term *immorality* was established by the Supreme Court of Pennsylvania in 1939. It was defined as "a course of conduct as offends the morals of the community and is a bad example to the youth whose ideals of a teacher is supposed to be fostered and elevated."[5]

Sexual Advances toward Students

Courts have left little doubt that they will deal judiciously with matters involving improper sexual conduct toward students. The courts support the general view that teaching is an *exemplary professional activity,* and those who teach should exhibit behavior that is above reproach in their dealings with students. Many state statutes include provisions that require teachers to impress on the minds of their students, principles of truth, morality, temperance, and humanity. These are very high standards that teachers are expected to meet in their professional roles. Given the position of the courts and the provisions in many state laws governing teacher conduct, it is not surprising to find that courts consistently uphold school districts when they produce evidence that a teacher has engaged in unlawful sexual involvement with students.

For example, a male teacher was dismissed for immoral conduct when he placed his hands inside the jeans of a student in the area of her buttocks and on other occasions squeezed the breast of a female student. The court determined the teacher's conduct to be grossly inappropriate.[6]

In another case, a male teacher was dismissed for professional misconduct when he tickled and touched female students on various parts of their bodies while engaged in a field trip experience. He also touched them between the legs. He was found lying on the bed with one of the female students watching television. The court determined that his activities were sufficient to sustain charges of unfitness to teach.[7]

A tenured art teacher was dismissed for immoral conduct when he placed his hands on female students by giving back rubs that resulted in further sexual contact. Evidence was also presented that he had engaged in sexual intercourse with two students at various places in the building.[8]

Other acts that have fallen under the category of immorality include *public sexual activity, unprofessional conduct, and criminal activity involving moral turpitude.* Any act or behavior that substantially interferes with the education of children and has a direct impact on the teacher's fitness to teach usually forms the basis for immorality charges. One fundamental issue courts seek to address is a determination of whether the teacher's alleged conduct adversely affects teaching performance and effectiveness. The response to this issue, in many cases, will determine whether a teacher should be dismissed.

GUIDES

Dismissal for Cause

1. School officials should avoid any actions regarding evaluation for dismissal that may be viewed as harassment or intimidation by the affected teacher.
2. School officials should be knowledgeable of their state's statutory definition of *insubordination* and ensure that cases involving insubordination are well documented. Professional disagreements between superiors and subordinates do not normally constitute insubordination.
3. Conviction of a felony or a series of misdemeanors may form grounds for dismissal and revocation of the teaching certificate.

4. Sexual misconduct by school personnel involving students will almost always result in dismissal and possible criminal charges.

FINANCIAL EXIGENCY (ABOLITION OF POSITIONS)

Financial exigency occurs when the district faces a bona fide reduction in its budget that results in abolishing certain employment positions. Positions may also be abolished when the district encounters reductions in student enrollment. The courts will generally support districts that demonstrate the need to reduce their teaching force, commonly called *reduction in force (RIF)*, when there is evidence that a legitimate financial problem exists. Obviously, districts should implement RIF policies and procedures that ensure that *substantive and procedural due process requirements* involving school personnel are met. Generally, these due process expectations are not as stringent, since dismissal decisions are based on financial concerns as opposed to personal or performance issues. The courts, in supporting financial exigency, usually require school districts to demonstrate the following:

1. A bona fide financial crises exists.
2. There is a rational relationship between the benefits derived from dismissal and the alleviation of the financial crises.
3. A fair and uniform set of due process procedures is followed in dismissal decisions.

School districts attempt to use objective criteria in building their reduction in force policies. Districts will generally use the following criteria in making RIF decisions:

1. Subject-matter needs
2. Teachers' length of experience (seniority) in the district
3. Teachers' length of experience in the teaching profession
4. Highest degree or certificate earned
5. Length of time in which the degree or certificate has been held
6. Subject-matter qualifications
7. Teaching performance

School districts typically attempt to achieve staff reduction through voluntary retirements, resignations, leaves of absence, and transfers. These areas should normally be addressed before action is taken to implement a RIF plan. Specific RIF policies and procedures should be reviewed by individuals teachers since there are variations among districts.

GUIDES

Financial Exigency

1. All employees affected by reduction in force must be afforded full due process provisions.
2. The burden of demonstrating bona fide financial exigency rests with the board of education.
3. School districts may not use financial exigency as a means to remove a teacher who has exercised a constitutionally protected right.
4. Seniority and job performance should receive priority in RIF decisions.
5. School district policy and/or state statute should be followed judiciously in implementing RIF policies.

Good or Just Cause

Just cause is designed to provide the district broader latitude in dismissing teachers for causes not specifically identified in state statutes. It is not designed to allow the district to dismiss a teacher for *personal, political, arbitrary, or capricious reasons.* The same due process provisions must be met under this category as would be met under the more specific causes for dismissal. So long as the board can justify its actions as being fair and reasonably related to a legitimate state interest, there should be no challenge by the courts. Just cause is not a category used frequently by school districts. Most tend to rely on the more specific causes previously identified.

Good or just cause may be used to bring dismissal charges against a teacher, particularly when there is a showing that performance and effectiveness are impaired and a question of fitness to teach arises as a major concern. Since this category is covered by many state statutes, school districts may use it so long as due process provisions are met. As with all charges, the burden of proof rests with school officials.

GUIDES

Good or Just Cause

1. Good or just cause provisions should not be used to arbitrarily dismiss a teacher from an employment position.

2. Good or just cause should never be motivated by actions that affect the constitutional protection rights of teachers such as free speech and association.
3. The burden of proof should always reside with school officials to demonstrate that just cause is valid.

COLLECTIVE BARGAINING

Collective bargaining has grown in popularity and appeal in public education. Although it has always provoked controversy, many educators view collective bargaining as a mechanism to achieve a greater role in management and operation of public schools. Since many of the issues involving collective bargaining focus on the rights of employees and the terms and conditions of employment, its very nature often evokes conflict and adversarial relationships between school boards and union representatives.

It is well recognized that collective bargaining has not always enjoyed the popularity it does today. In fact, it did not gain legal protection until the early 1930s in the private sector. The evolution of this concept in the public sector developed very slowly, due primarily to the belief and acceptance of governmental sovereignty. Public schools, as agents of the state, exerted almost complete control of school operations as well as terms and conditions of employment consistent with their state's statutory mandates and local district policy. There was a prevailing view among state lawmakers that this sovereign power should not be abrogated.

Collective bargaining gradually emerged in the public sector in the late 1940s when Wisconsin became one of the first states to enact legislation allowing bargaining to occur. However, it was not until the decade of the 1960s that teachers launched a major effort to gain a greater level of involvement in the administration and operations of their schools. Most states currently permit some form of bargaining between teachers and school boards. These agreements may vary from required bargaining to some form of *meet and confer provision*.

Irrespective of these variations, the basic intent is to create teacher empowerment and shared power between teachers and school boards. Obviously, some states are more liberal than others in deciding on items that are negotiable. For example, arbitration is mandated in some states but prohibited in others. In any case, the primary objective is to create conditions where school employees are afforded the opportunity to affiliate with a union without fear of reprisal for their participation. One common element found in most state statutes is a *good faith* requirement imposed on employers, which implies that they must bargain with the recognized bargaining unit with the sincere intent to reach a reasonable agreement. In fact, this good faith provision affects both parties during the bargaining process.

Private Sector versus Public Sector Bargaining

There are obvious differences between private sector and public sector bargaining. One of the most notable differences is that private sector employees do not enjoy constitutional protections as do public sector employees. Public sector employees are afforded equal protection rights under due process as well as certain rights enacted by state statutes for their protection.

Private sector rights were severely restructured in 1947 with an amendment to the National Labor Relations Act (NLRA), which had passed in 1935 to support collective bargaining as an effort to improve management and labor relations. The National Labor Relations Board was formed during this time to remedy unfair labor practices. With the amendments to the NLRA, limitations were imposed on various union practices after widespread evidence of union corruption surfaced. The amended version resulted in the Labor Management Relations Act, commonly called the Taft-Hartley Act. This act was subsequently amended in 1959 with the Labor Management Reporting and Disclosure Act (LMRDA), which provided protection to private sector employees who faced various forms of union abuse. It also invoked penalties for misappropriation of union funds.

Another significant difference is that, in many instances, public school teachers are not permitted to strike. Proponents of public sector negotiations view this restriction as a real limitation in the sense that bargaining strength is weakened regarding the capacity to reject the terms and conditions offered during the negotiation process. In the private sector, rejection of an offer is most often followed by a strike when an impasse occurs. In states where strikes are not permitted by law, penalties are imposed on teachers and union officials, which may range from loss of salary to dismissal for teachers and stiff fines for union officials. When an impasse occurs, public sector bargaining is also impacted by state and local budget restraints. Since funding is determined by state legislatures and dependent on tax projections and revenue, regulations regarding salary issues are limited by state appropriations to education, irrespective of bargaining agreements.

State Involvement

A number of states have passed permissive legislation to aid recognized union organizations. Some states support an *agency shop* measure, stipulating that teachers must be members in good standing with the union through dues payment, or some form of service charge, if the teachers are not affiliated with the recognized bargaining unit. A few state laws make union affiliation mandatory for teachers as a condition to continuing their employment. This agreement is commonly referred to as *union shop*. Other states require teachers to affiliate with the recognized bargaining unit when they make application for a teaching position. This arrangement is commonly referred to as the *closed shop*. Still other states have enacted legislation that protects employers from harassment by employers and union officials because they elect not to affiliate with the bargaining unit. When a bargaining unit is granted the exclusive right to represent employees, it must do so on a fair and equitable basis, irrespective of whether the employee is a member or not. State law in most cases will require the union to do so.

Scope of Collective Bargaining

State laws vary regarding issues that are deemed negotiable. These issues normally fall under the categories of mandatory, permissive, and illegal. Issues pertaining to working conditions involving length of the work day, teaching workload, extra duty assignments, leaves of absences, and other fringe benefits are almost always considered *mandatory*, which means that there must be bargaining issues involving both parties. *Permissive* subjects are generally based on common agreement between both parties and would not constitute a breach of duty to bargain in good faith. Issues involving personnel recruitment, selection, and induction are considered administrative prerogatives not subject to mandatory negotiations. Since these areas vary among states, there is an obvious lack of a clear distinction among these areas.

In areas involving mandatory bargaining, school boards are required to operate in good faith bargaining. As previously indicated, state statutes establish the framework regarding the scope of collective negotiations in public schools. Several basic issues emerge in relation to negotiation agreements. These normally cover areas that a school board can negotiate as well as those in which it cannot negotiate. Also covered are issues that must be negotiated until agreement is reached by both parties. There are issues that are not mandatory or permissive in some states. They are a function of negotiations between the teacher's union and the school board. These have included areas such as the teachers' planning periods, changes in the length of class periods, nonteaching assignments, sick leave banks, academic policies, and many other areas.

Although there are variations among the states regarding negotiable items, there is a great deal of consistency with respect to managerial prerogatives that must remain under the purview of the school board.[9]

Impasse and Bargaining

On numerous occasions, the parties involved in negotiations fail to reach an agreement, and it becomes obvious that no further progress is possible toward resolution. When this occurs, an *impasse* has emerged. The regular negotiation process calls for a series of options designed to resolve the dispute. These options are as follows:

1. *Mediation* occurs when a neutral party is engaged to assist both parties in reaching objective solutions to the dispute at hand. The mediation is normally chosen by common agreement between parties. If mediation fails, another option is to engage a fact-finder.
2. A *fact-finder* is a third party who attempts to analyze facts and determine where compromise might occur. The fact-finder offers solutions that are not binding on either party. If the fact-finding process fails to resolve the dispute, the final step involves arbitration.
3. *Arbitration* occurs when a third party performs similar functions to those performed by the fact-finder. If the arbitration is *binding*, then what is recommended as a resolution to the dispute is binding on both parties.

Workers' Compensation

Teachers in most states are protected by workers' compensation when they receive injury during the course of performing their professional duties. The theory supporting workers' compensation is that the employing agency should assume responsibility for injury suffered by employees during the conduct of the agency's business. Workers' compensation does not normally apply in situations where an employee is willfully or wrongfully injured by the employer or a colleague. The injured employee does not need to prove that any injury resulted from a certain incident.

In recent years, increased flexibility and latitude have been provided in allowing compensation for a job-related injury that developed over a period of time. For example, a teacher might incur an injury over a period of time for lifting heavy equipment or performing routine tasks such as rearranging furniture in the classroom. In some instances, an employee is covered by workers' compensation if he or she aggravates a preexisting condition. In all cases, there must be supportive evidence that the injury grew out of the execution of professional duties and responsibilities.

It is very difficult, in most instances, to receive coverage for psychological or mental illness unless the employee can adequately demonstrate that he or she was involved in an unusually and unavoidable stressful work environment. An employee will not normally succeed in cases of self-induced stress that grows out of his or her ineffectiveness in performing expected job duties and responsibilities.

Most states have explicit processes and procedures that employees must follow to receive workers' compensation, including a specified time in which the injury must be reported, in injury situations covered by state statutes. Virtually every state has an agency that administers the program. As a last resort, employees may resort to the courts in cases where they are denied workers' compensation benefits once the state's procedures have been exhausted.

GUIDES

Collective Bargaining

1. The collective negotiations process should always be guided by a good faith effort involving both parties—school boards and union officials.
2. School boards should not negotiate items for which they have no legal authority, such as salary increases and employment of personnel, unless there is expressed statutory authority to do so.
3. Any sustained action taken by striking teachers that may disrupt educational opportunities for students will not likely receive court support.
4. Constitutionally protected rights and freedoms of teachers should not be impaired by collective bargaining agreements.

5. Teachers are protected by workers' compensation when they receive job-related injuries.

ENDNOTES

1. *Pickering v. Board of Education,* 225 N.E. 2d, 16 (Ill. 1967).
2. *Blaine v. Moffat County School District Region No. 1,* 748 p.2d 1280 (Colo. 1998).
3. *Sanders v. Board of Education of South Sioux Community School District No. 11,* 263 N.W. 2d 461, Neb. (1978).
4. *Thompson v. Southwest School District,* 483 F.Supp. 1170 (Mo. 1980).
5. *Horosko v. Mt. Pleasant School District,* 335. Pa. 369 6 A.2d 866 (1939). Cert denied 308 U.S. 553 (1939).
6. *Fadler v. Illinois State Board of Education,* 153 Ill. App. 3d 1024, 106 Ill. 840 506 N.E. 2d 640 (5 Dist. 1987).
7. *Weissman v. Board of Education of Jefferson County School District No. R-1,* 190 Colo. 414, 547 P.2d 1267 (1976).
8. *Johnson v. Beaverhead City High School District,* 236 Mont. 532, 771 P.2d 137 (1989).
9. *Rochester Area School District v. Rochester Education Association,* No. 2915 C.D. 1999 (Pa. Commw. Ct. 2000).

APPENDIX

A

Selected Constitutional Provisions

The Constitution of the United States and selected key provisions and amendments affecting education.

CONSTITUTION OF THE UNITED STATES

We the People of the United States, in Order to form a more perfect Union, establish Justice, insure domestic Tranquility, provide for the common defence, promote the general Welfare, and secure the Blessings of Liberty to ourselves and our Posterity, do ordain and establish this Constitution for the United States of America.

Article I.

Section 1. All legislative Powers herein granted shall be vested in a Congress of the United States, which shall consist of a Senate and House of Representatives.

Section 2. The House of Representatives shall be composed of Members chosen every second Year by the People of the several States, and the Electors in each State shall have the Qualifications requisite for Electors of the most numerous Branch of the State Legislature. . . .

Section 7. All Bills for raising Revenue shall originate in the House of Representatives; but the Senate may propose or concur with amendments as on other Bills.

Every Bill which shall have passed the House of Representatives and the Senate, shall, before it become a Law, be presented to the President of the United States; If he approve he shall sign it, but if not he shall return it, with his Objections to that House in which it shall have originated, who shall enter the Objections at large on their Journal, and proceed to reconsider it. If after such Reconsideration two thirds of that House shall agree to pass the Bill, it shall be sent, together with the Objections, to the other House, by which it shall likewise be reconsidered, and if approved by two thirds of that House, it shall become a Law. But in all such Cases the Votes of both Houses shall be determined by yeas and Nays, and the Names of the Persons voting for and against the Bill shall be entered on the Journal of each House respectively. If any Bill shall not be returned by the President within ten Days (Sunday excepted) after it shall have been presented to him, the Same shall be a Law, in like Manner as if he had signed it, unless the Congress by their Adjournment prevents its Return, in which Case it shall not be a Law.

Article II.

Section 1. The executive Power shall be vested in a President of the United States of America. . . .

Section 2. The President shall be Commander in Chief of the Army and Navy of the United States, and of the Militia of the several states, . . .

He shall Power, by and with the Advice and Consent of the Senate, to make Treaties, provided two thirds of the Senators present concur; and he shall nominate, and by and with the Advice and Consent of the Senate, shall appoint Ambassadors, other public Ministers and Consuls, Judges of the supreme Court, and all other Officers of the United States, whose Appointments are not herein otherwise provided for, and which shall be established by Law: but the Congress may by Law vest the Appointment of such inferior Officers, as they think proper, in the President alone, in the Courts of Law, or in the Heads of Departments. . . .

Section 4. The United States shall guarantee to every State in this Union a Republican Form of Government, and shall protect each of them against Invasion; and on Application of the Legislature, or of the Executive (when the Legislature cannot be convened) against domestic Violence.

Article III.

Section 1. The judicial Power of the United States, shall be vested in one supreme Court, and in such inferior Courts as the Congress may from time to time ordain and establish. The Judges, both of the supreme and inferior Courts, shall hold their Offices during good Behaviour, and shall, at stated

Times, receive for their Services, a Compensation, which shall not be diminished during their Continuance in Office.

Section 2. The judicial Power shall extend to all Cases, in Law and Equity, arising under this Constitution, the Laws of the United States, and Treaties made, or which shall be made, under their Authority;—to all Cases affecting Ambassadors, other public Ministers and Consuls;—to all Cases of admiralty and maritime Jurisdiction;—to Controversies to which the United States shall be a Party;—to Controversies between two or more States;—between a State and Citizens of another State;—between Citizens of different States;—between Citizens of the same State claiming Lands under Grants of different States, and between a State, or the Citizens thereof, and foreign States, Citizens or Subjects. . . .

The Trial of all Crimes, except in Cases of Impeachment, shall be by Jury; and such Trial shall be held in the State where the said Crimes shall have been committed; but when not committed within any State, the Trial shall be at such Place or Places as the Congress may by Law have directed.

Article IV.

Section 1. Full Faith and Credit shall be given in each State to the public Acts, Records, and judicial Proceedings of every other State. And the Congress may by general Laws prescribe the Manner in which such Acts, Records and Proceedings shall be proved, and the Effect thereof.

Section 2. The Citizens of each State shall be entitled to all Privileges and Immunities of the Citizens in the several States.

Article V.

The Congress, whenever two thirds of both Houses shall deem it necessary, shall propose Amendments to this Constitution, or, on the Application of the Legislatures of two thirds of the several States, shall call a Convention for proposing Amendments, which, in either Case, shall be valid to all Intents and Purposes, as Part of this Constitution, when ratified by the Legislatures of three fourths of the several States, or by Conventions in three fourths thereof, as the one or the other Mode of Ratification may be proposed by the Congress; Provided that no Amendment which may be made prior to the Year One thousand eight hundred and eight shall in any Manner affect the first and fourth Clauses in the Ninth

Section of the first Article; and that no State, without its Consent, shall be deprived of it's equal Suffrage in the Senate. . . .

This Constitution, and the Laws of the United which shall be made in Pursuance thereof; and all Treaties made, or which shall be made, under the Authority of the United States, shall be the supreme Law of the Land; and the Judges in every State shall be found thereby, any Thing in the Constitution or Laws of any State to the Contrary notwithstanding.

The Senators and Representatives before mentioned, and the Members of the several State Legislatures, and all executive and judicial Officers, both of the United States and of the several States, shall be bound by Oath or Affirmation, to support this Constitution; but no religious Test shall ever be required as a qualification to any office or public trust under the United States.

Article VII.

The Ratification of the Conventions of nine States, shall be sufficient for the Establishment of this Constitution between the States so ratifying the Same.

AMENDMENTS TO THE CONSTITUTION OF THE UNITED STATES OF AMERICA

Articles in Addition to, and Amendment of, the Constitution of the United States of America, Proposed by Congress, and Ratified by the Several States, Pursuant to the Fifth Article of the Original Constitution

Amendment [I.] [1791]

Congress shall make no law respecting an establishment of religion, or prohibiting the free exercise of thereof; or abridging the freedom of speech, or of the press; or the right of the people peaceably to assemble, and to petition the Government for a redress of grievances. . . .

Amendment [IV.] [1791]

The right of the people to be secure in their persons, houses, papers, and effects, against unreasonable searches and seizures, shall not be violated, and no Warrants shall issue, but upon probable cause, supported by Oath or affirmation, and particularly describing the place to be searched, and the persons or things to be seized.

Amendment [V.] [1791]

No person shall be held to answer for a capital, or otherwise infamous crime, unless on a presentment or indictment of a Grand Jury, except in cases arising in the land or naval forces, or in the Militia, when in actual service in time of War or public danger; nor shall any person be subject for the same offence to be twice put in jeopardy of life or limb; nor shall be compelled in any criminal case to be a witness against himself, nor be deprived of life, liberty, or property, without due process of law; nor shall private property be taken for public use, without just compensation. . . .

Amendment [VIII.] [1791]

Excessive bail shall not be required, nor excessive fines imposed, nor cruel and unusual punishments inflicted.

Amendment [IX.] [1791]

The enumeration in the Constitution, of certain rights, shall not be construed to deny or disparage others retained by the people.

Amendment [X.] [1791]

The powers not delegated to the United States by the Constitution, nor prohibited by it to the States, are reserved to the States respectively, or to the people. . . .

Amendment [XIV.] [1868]

Section 1. All persons born or naturalized in the United States and subject to the jurisdiction thereof, are citizens of the United States and of the State wherein they reside. No State shall make or enforce any law which shall abridge the privileges or immunities of citizens of the United States; or shall any State deprive any person of life, liberty, or property, without due process of law; nor deny to any person within its jurisdiction the equal protection of the laws.

Section 5. The Congress shall have power to enforce, by appropriate legislation, the provisions of this article.

B

Selected Federal Statutes

CIVIL RIGHTS ACTS OF 1866, 1870—42 U.S.C.§ 1981

Section 1981 provides: "*All persons* within the jurisdiction of the United States shall have the same right . . . *to make and enforce contracts,* to sue, be parties, give evidence, and to the full and equal benefit of all laws and proceedings for the security of persons and property as is enjoyed by white citizens, and shall be subject to like punishments, pains, penalties, taxes, licenses, and exactions of every kind, and to no other."

CIVIL RIGHTS ACT OF 1871— 42 U.S.C. § 1983

Section 1983 provides: "Every person who, under color of any statute, ordinance, regulation, custom or usage, of any State or Territory, subjects, or causes to be subjected, any citizen of the United States or other person within the jurisdiction thereof to the *deprivation of any rights,* privileges or immunities *secured by the Constitution and laws,* shall be liable to the party injured in an action at law, suit in equity, or other proper proceeding for redress."

CIVIL RIGHTS ACT OF 1964 TITLE VII (SELECTED PARTS) 42 U.S.C.A. § 2000E—E—2

EQUAL EMPLOYMENT OPPORTUNITIES
§ 2000e—2. Unlawful employment practices

Employer practices

(a) It shall be an unlawful employment practice for an employer—

(1) to fail or refuse to hire or to discharge any individual, or otherwise to discriminate against any individual with respect to his compensation, terms, conditions, or privileges of employment, because of such individual's race, color, religion, sex, or national origin; or

(2) to limit, segregate, or classify his employees or applicants for employment in any way which would deprive or tend to deprive any individual of employment opportunities or otherwise adversely affect his status as an employee, because of such individual's race, color, religion, sex, or national origin.

Employment agency practices

(b) It shall be an unlawful employment practice for an employment agency to fail or refuse to refer for employment, or otherwise to discriminate against, any individual because of his race, color, religion, sex, or national origin, or to classify or refer for employment any individual on the basis of his race, color, religions, sex, or national origin. . . .

Training programs

(d) It shall be an unlawful employment practice for any employer, labor organization, or joint labor-management committee controlling apprenticeship or other training or retraining, including on-the-job training programs to discriminate against any individual because of his race, color, religion, sex, or national origin in admission to, or employment in, any program established to provide apprenticeship or other training.

Business or enterprises with personnel qualified on basis of religion, sex, or national origin; educational institutions with personnel of particular religion

(e) Notwithstanding any other provision of this subchapter, (1) it shall not be an unlawful employment practice for an employer to hire and employ employees, for an employment agency to classify, or refer for employment any individual, for a labor organization to classify its membership or to classify or refer for employment any individual, or for an employer, labor organization, or joint labor-management committee controlling apprenticeship or other training or retraining programs to admit or employ any individual in any such program, on the basis of his religion, sex, or national origin in those certain instances where religion, sex, or national origin is a bona fide occupational qualification reasonably necessary to the normal operation of that particular business or enterprise, and (2) it shall not be an unlawful employment practice for a school, college, university, or other educational institution or institution of learning to hire and employ employees of a particular religion if such school, college, university, or other educational institution or institution of learning is, in whole or in substantial part, owned, supported, controlled, or managed by a particular religion or by a particular religious corporation, association, or society, or if the curriculum of such school, college, university, or other educational institution or institution of learning is directed toward the propagation of a particular religion. . . .

Senior or merit system; quantity or quality of production; ability tests; compensation based on sex and authorized by minimum wage provisions

(h) Notwithstanding any other provision of this subchapter, it shall not be an unlawful employment practice for an employer to apply different standards of compensation, or different terms, conditions, or privileges of employment pursuant to a bona fide seniority or merit system, or a system which measures earnings by quantity or quality of production or to employees who work in different locations, provided that such differences are not the result of an intention to discriminate because of race, color, religion, sex, or national origin, nor shall it be an unlawful employment practice for an employer to give and to act upon the results of any professionally developed ability test provided that such test, its administration or action upon the results is not designed, intended, or used to discriminate because of race, color, religion, sex or national origin. It shall not be an unlawful employment practice under this subchapter for any employer to differentiate upon the basis of sex in determining the amount of the wages or compensation paid or to be paid to employees of such employer if such differentiation is authorized by the provisions of section 206(d) of Title 29. . . .

Preferential treatment not to be granted on account of existing number or percentage imbalance

(j) Nothing contained in this subchapter shall be interpreted to require any employer, employment agency, labor organization, or joint labor-management committee subject to this subchapter to grant preferential treatment to any individual or to any group because of the race, color, religion, sex, or national origin of such individual or group on account of an imbalance which may exist with respect to the total number or percentage of persons of any race, color, religion, sex, or national origin employed by any employer, referred or classified for employment by any employment agency or labor organization, admitted to membership or classified by any labor organization, or admitted to, or employed in, any apprenticeship or other training program, in comparison with the total number or percentage of persons of such race, color, religion, sex, or national origin in any community, State, section, or other area, or in the available work force in any community, State, section, or other area.

Pub.L. 88-352, Title VII, § 703, July 2, 1964, 78 Stat. 255; Pub.L. 92-261, § 8(a), (b), Mar. 24, 1972, 86 Stat. 109.

Education amendments of 1972, Title IX—20 U.S.C. § 1681

Section 901 of Title IX provides in part:

(A) *No person* . . . shall, on the basis of *sex,* be excluded from participation in, be denied the benefits of, or be subjected to discrimination under any *education program* or activity *receiving Federal financial assistance,* except that:

(1) in regard to admissions . . .

(3) this section *shall not apply* to an educational institution which is controlled by a religious organization if the application . . . would not be consistent *with the religious tenets* of such organization. . . .

Title IX regulations provide in part:

"Nondiscrimination on the Basis of Sex in Education Programs and Activities; Receiving or Benefiting from Federal Financial Assistance" 34 C.F.R. § 106.1-106.71

Title IX Regulations, 34 C.F.R. § 106-1 et seq.

Subpart C—Discrimination on the Basis of Sex in Admission and Recruitment Prohibited

§ 106.21   Admission

(a) *General.* No person shall, on the basis of sex, be denied admission, or be subjected to discrimination in admission . . .

(b) *Specific prohibitions.*

(1) [a] recipient . . . shall not:

(i) Give preference to one person over another on the basis of sex, by ranking applicants separately on such basis . . .

(ii) Apply numerical limitations upon the number or proportion of persons of either sex who may be admitted . . .

(2) A recipient shall not administer . . . any test . . . for admission which has a disproportionately adverse effect on persons on the basis of sex unless the use of such test . . . is shown to predict valid success in the education program or activity in question and alternative tests . . . which do not have such a disproportionately adverse effect are shown to be unavailable.

(c) *Prohibitions relating to marital or parental status* . . . a recipient . . . :

(1) Shall not apply any rule concerning . . . parental, family, or marital status . . . which treats persons differently on the basis of sex . . .

(3) Shall treat disabilities related to pregnancy, childbirth, termination of pregnancy, or recovery therefrom in the same manner . . . as any other temporary disability . . . and

(4) Shall not make pre-admission inquiry as to the marital status of an applicant for admission, . . .

Subpart D—Discrimination on the Basis of Sex in Education Programs and Activities Prohibited

§ 106.31 Education Programs and Activities

(a) *General.* Except as provided elsewhere in this part, no person shall, on the basis of sex, be excluded from participation in, be denied the benefits of, or be subjected to discrimination under any academic, extracurricular, research, occupational training, or other education program or activity operated by a recipient which receives or benefits from Federal financial assistance . . .

(b) *Specific prohibitions.* Except as provided in this subpart, in providing any aid, benefit, or service to a student, a recipient shall not on the basis of sex . . .

(2) Provide different aid, benefits, or services or provide aid, benefits, or services in a different manner . . .

(4) Subject any person to separate or different rules of behavior, sanctions, or other treatment . . .

§ 106.34 Access to Course Offerings

A recipient shall not provide any course or otherwise carry out any of its education program or activity separately on the basis of sex . . .

(b) This section does not prohibit grouping of students in physical education classes and activities by ability as assessed by objective standards of individual performance developed and applied without regard to sex.

(c) This section does not prohibit separation of students by sex within physical education classes or activities during participation in wrestling, boxing, rugby, ice hockey, football, basketball and other sports the purpose or major activity of which involves bodily contact.

(d) Where use of a single standard of measuring skill or progress in a physical education class has an adverse effect on members of one sex, the recipient shall use appropriate standards which do not have such effect.

(e) Portions of classes in elementary and secondary schools which deal exclusively with human sexuality may be conducted in separate sessions for boys and girls.

(f) Recipients may make requirements based on vocal range or quality which may result in a chorus or choruses of one or predominantly one sex.

§ 106.36   Counseling and Use of Appraisal and Counseling Materials

(a) *Counseling.* A recipient shall not discriminate against any person on the basis of sex in the counseling or guidance of students or applicants for admission.

(b) *Use of appraisal and counseling materials.* A recipient which uses testing or other materials for appraising or counseling students shall not use different materials for students on the basis of their sex or use materials which permit or require different treatment of students on such basis unless such different materials cover the same occupations and interest areas and the use of such different materials is shown to be essential to eliminate sex bias. . . . Where the use of a counseling test or other instrument results in a substantially disproportionate number of members of one sex in any particular course of study or classification, the recipient shall take such action as is necessary to assure itself that such disproportion is not the result of discrimination in the instrument or its application.

(c) *Disproportion in classes.* Where a recipient finds that a particular class contains a substantially disproportionate number of individuals of one sex, the recipient shall take such action as is necessary to assure itself that such disproportion is not the result of discrimination on the basis of sex in counseling or appraisal materials or by counselors.

§ 106.40   Marital or Parental Status

(a) *Status generally.* A recipient shall not apply any rule concerning a student's actual or potential parental, family, or marital status which treats students differently on the basis of sex.

(b) *Pregnancy and related conditions.* (1) A recipient shall not discriminate against any student, or exclude any student from its education program or activity, including any class or extracurricular activity, on the basis of such student's pregnancy, childbirth, false pregnancy, termination of pregnancy or recovery therefrom, unless the student requests voluntarily to participate in a separate portion of the program or activity of the recipient.

(2) A recipient may require such a student to obtain the certification of a physician that the student is physically and emotionally able to continue participation in the normal education program or activity. . . .

(3) A recipient which operates a portion of its education program or activity separately for pregnant students, admittance to which is completely voluntary on the part of the student . . . shall ensure that the instructional program in the separate program is comparable to that offered to non-pregnant students.

(4) A recipient shall treat pregnancy, childbirth, false pregnancy, termination of pregnancy and recovery therefrom in the same manner and under the same policies as any other temporary disability with respect to any medical or hospital benefit, service, plan or policy which such recipient administers, operates . . . with respect to students. . . .

DISCRIMINATION BASED ON SEX TITLE IX (SELECTED PARTS) 20 U.S.C.A. § 1681

§ 1861. Sex

Prohibition against discrimination; exceptions

(a) No person in the United States shall, on the basis of sex, be excluded from participation in, be denied the benefits of, or be subjected to discrimination under any education program or activity receiving Federal financial assistance, except that:

Classes of educational institutions subject to prohibition

(1) in regard to admissions to educational institutions, this section shall apply only to institutions of vocational education, professional education, and graduate higher education, and to public institutions of undergraduate higher education;

Educational institutions commencing planned change in admissions

(2) in regard to admissions to educational institutions, this section shall not apply (A) for one year from June 23, 1972, nor for six years after June 23, 1972, in the case of an educational institution which has begun the process of changing from being an institution which admits only students of one sex to being an institution which admits students of both sexes, but only if it is carrying out a plan for such a change which is approved by the Commissioner of Education or (B) for sever years from the date an educational institution begins the process of changing from being an institution which admits only students of only one sex to being an institution which admits students of both sexes, but only if it is carrying out a plan for such a change which is approved by the Commissioner of Education, whichever is the later;

Educational institutions of religious organizations with contrary religious tenets

(3) this section shall not apply to an educational institution which is controlled by a religious organization if the application of this subsection would not be consistent with the religious tenets of such organization;

Educational institutions training individuals for military services or merchant marine

(4) this section shall not apply to an educational institution whose primary purpose is the training of individuals for the military services of the United States, or the merchant marine;

Public educational institutions with traditional and continuing admissions policy

(5) in regard to admissions this section shall not apply to any public institution of undergraduate higher education which is an institution that traditionally and continually from its es-

tablishment has had a policy of admitting only students of one sex;

Social fraternities or sororities; voluntary youth service organizations

(6) this section shall not apply to membership practices—

(A) of a social fraternity or social sorority which is exempt from taxation under section 501(a) of Title 26, the active membership of which consists primarily of students in attendance at an institution of higher education, or

(B) of the Young Men's Christian Association, Young Women's Christian Association, Girl Scouts, Boy Scouts, Camp Fire Girls, and voluntary youth service organizations which are so exempt, the membership of which has traditionally been limited to persons of one sex and principally to persons of less than nineteen years of age;

Boy or girl conferences

(7) this section shall not apply to—

(A) any program or activity of the American Legion undertaken in connection with the organization or operation of any Boys State conference, Boys Nation conference, Girls State conference, or Girls Nation conference; or

(B) any program or activity of any secondary school or educational institution specifically for—

(i) the promotion of any Boys State conference, Boys Nation conference, Girls State conference, or Girls Nation conference; or

(ii) the selection of students to attend any such conference;

Father-son or mother-daughter activities at educational institutions

(8) this section shall not preclude father-son or mother-daughter activities at an educational institution, but if such activities are provided for students of one sex, opportunities for reasonably comparable activities shall be provided for students of the other sex; and

Institution of higher education scholarship awards in "beauty" pageants

(9) this section shall not apply with respect to any scholarship or other financial assistance awarded by an institution of

higher education to any individual because such individual has received such award in any pageant in which the attainment of such award is based upon a combination of factors related to the personal appearance, poise, and talent of such individual and in which participation is limited to individuals of one sex only, so long as such pageant is in compliance with other non-discrimination provisions of Federal law.

Preferential or disparate treatment because of imbalance in participation or receipt of Federal benefits; statistical evidence of imbalance

(b) Nothing contained in subsection (a) of this section shall be interpreted to require any educational institution to grant preferential or disparate treatment to the members of one sex on account of an imbalance which may exist with respect to the total number of percentage of persons of that sex participating in or receiving the benefits of any federally supported program or activity, in comparison with the total number or percentage of persons of that sex in any community, State, section, or other area: *Provided,* That this subsection shall not be construed to prevent the consideration in any hearing or proceeding under this chapter of statistical evidence tending to show that such an imbalance exists with respect to the participation in, or receipt of the benefits of, any such program or activity by the members of one sex.

Educational institution defined

(c) For purposes of this chapter an educational institution means any public or private preschool, elementary, or secondary school, or any institution of vocational, professional, or higher education, except that in the case of an educational institution composed of more than one school, college, or department which are administratively separate units, such term means each such school, college, or department.

Pub.L. 92–318, Title IX, § 901, June 23, 1972, 86 Stat. 373; Pub.L. 93–568, § 3(a), Dec. 31, 1974, 88 Stat. 1862; Pub.L. 94–482, Title IV, § 412(a), Oct. 12, 1976, 90 Stat. 2234.

FAMILY RIGHTS AND PRIVACY ACT (BUCKLEY AMENDMENT) (SELECTED PARTS) 20 U.S.C.A. § 1232G

§ 1232G. Family Educational and Privacy Rights

Conditions for availability of funds to educational agencies or institutions; inspection and review of education records; specific information to be made available; procedure for access to education records; reasonableness of time for such access; hearings; written explanations by parents; definitions

(a)(1)(A) No funds shall be made available under any applicable program to any educational agency or institution which has a policy of denying, or which effectively prevents, the parents of students who are or have been in attendance at a school of such agency or at such institution, as the case may be, the right to inspect and review the education records of their children. If any material or document in the education record of a student includes information on more than one student, the parents of one of such students shall have the right to inspect and review only such part of such material or document as relates to such student or to be informed of the specific information contained in such part of such material. Each educational agency or institution shall establish appropriate procedures for the granting of a request by parents for access to the education records of their children within a reasonable period of time, but in no case more than forty-five days after the request has been made. . . .

(2) No funds shall be made available under any applicable program to any educational agency or institution unless the parents of students who are or have been in attendance at a school of such agency or at such institution are provided an opportunity for a hearing by such agency or institution, in accordance with regulations of the Secretary, to challenge the content of such student's education records, in order to insure that the records are not inaccurate, misleading, or otherwise in violation of the privacy or other rights of students, and to provide an opportunity for the correction or deletion of any such inaccurate, misleading, or otherwise inappropriate data contained therein and to insert into such records a written explanation of the parents respecting the content of such records. . . .

Release of education records; parental consent requirement; exceptions; compliance with judicial orders and subpoenas; audit and evaluation of Federally-supported education programs; record-keeping

(b)(1) No funds shall be made available under any applicable program to any educational agency or institution which has a policy or practice of permitting the release of education records (or personally identifiable information contained therein other than directory information, as defined in paragraph (5) of subsection (a) of this section) of students without the written consent of their parents to any individual, agency, or organization, other than to the following—

(A) other school officials, including teachers within the educational institution or local educational agency who have been determined by such agency or institution to have legitimate educational interests;

(B) officials of other schools or school systems in which the student seeks or intends to enroll, upon condition that the student's parents be notified of the transfer, receive a copy of the record if desired, and have an opportunity for a hearing to challenge the content of the record;

(C) authorized representatives of (i) the Comptroller General of the United States, (ii) the Secretary, (iii) an administrative head of an education agency (as defined in section 1221e—3(c) of this title), or (iv) State educational authorities, under the conditions set forth in paragraph (3) of this subsection;

(D) in connection with a student's application for, or receipt of, financial aid;

(E) State and local officials or authorities to whom such information is specifically required to be reported or disclosed pursuant to state statute adopted prior to November 19, 1974;

(F) organizations conducting studies for, or on behalf of, educational agencies or institutions for the purpose of developing, validating, or administering predictive tests, administering student aid programs, and improving instruction, if such studies are conducted in such a manner as will not permit the personal identification of students and their parents by persons other than representatives of such organizations and such information will be destroyed when no longer needed for the purpose for which it is conducted;

(G) accrediting organizations in order to carry out their accrediting functions;

(H) parents of a dependent student of such parents, as defined in section 152 of Title 26; and

(I) subject to regulations of the Secretary, in connection with an emergency, appropriate persons if the knowledge of such information is necessary to protect the health or safety of the student or other persons. Nothing in clause (E) of this paragraph shall prevent a State from further limiting the number or type of State or local officials who will continue to have access thereunder.

(2) No funds shall be made available under any applicable program to any educational agency or institution which has a policy or practice of releasing, or providing access to, any personally identifiable information in education records other than directory information, or as is permitted under paragraph (1) of this subsection unless—

(A) there is written consent from the student's parents specifying records to be released, the reasons for such release, and to whom, and with a copy of the records to be released to the student's parents and the student if desired by the parents, or

(B) such information is furnished in compliance with judicial order, or pursuant to any lawfully issued subpoena, upon condition that parents and the students are notified of all such orders or subpoenas in advance of the compliance therewith by the educational institution or agency. . . .

(C) With respect to this subsection, personal information shall only be transferred to a third party on the condition that such party will not permit any other party to have access to such information without the written consent of the parents of the student. . . .

Students' rather than parents' permission or consent

(d) For the purposes of this section, whenever a student has attained eighteen years of age, or is attending an institution of postsecondary education the permission or consent required of and the rights accorded to the parents of the student shall thereafter only be required of and accorded to the student. . . .

Pub.L. 90–247, Title IV, § 438, as added Pub.L. 93–380, Title V. § 513(a), Aug. 21, 1974, 88 Stat. 572, and amended Pub.L. 93–568 § 2(a), Dec. 31, 1974, 88 Stat. 1858.

§ 1232H. Protection of Pupil Rights

Inspection by parents or guardians of instructional material

(a) All instructional material, including teacher's manuals, films, tapes, or other supplementary instructional material which will be used in connection with any research or experimentation program or project shall be available for inspection by the parents or guardians of the children engaged in such program or project. For the purpose of this section "research or experimentation program or project: research means any program or project in any applicable program designed to explore or develop new or unproven teaching methods or techniques.

Psychiatric or psychological examinations, testing, or treatment

(b) No student shall be required, as part of any applicable program, to submit to psychiatric examination, testing, or treatment, or psychological examination, testing, or treatment, in which the primary purpose is to reveal information concerning:

(1) political affiliations;

(2) mental and psychological problems potentially embarrassing to the student or his family;

(3) sex behavior and attitudes;

(4) illegal, anti-social, self-incriminating, and demeaning behavior;

(5) critical appraisals of other individuals with whom respondents have close family relationships;

(6) legally recognized privileged and analogous relationships, such as those of lawyers, physicians, and ministers; or;

(7) income (other than that required by law to determine eligibility for participation in a program or for receiving financial assistance under such program), without the prior consent of the student (if the student is an adult or emancipated minor), or in the case of unemancipated minor, without the prior written consent of the parent.

(Jan. 2, 1968, P.L. 90–247, Title IV, Part C, Subpart 2, § 439, as added Aug. 21, 1974, P.L. 93–380, Title V, § 514 (a), 88 Stat. 574; Nov. 1, 1978, P.L. 95–561, Title XII, Part D, § 1250, 92 Stat. 2355.)

AMERICANS WITH DISABILITIES ACT OF 1990 (SELECTED PARTS), PUBLIC LAW 101–336, 42 U.S.C. § 12101

Title I—Employment

§ 101. Definitions

As used in this title:

(1) Commission.—The term "Commission" means the Equal Employment Opportunity Commission established by section 705 of the Civil Rights Act of 1964 (42 U.S.C. 2000e—4).

(2) Covered entity.—The term "covered entity" means an employer, employment agency, labor organization, or joint labor-management committee.

(3) Direct threat.—The term "direct threat" means a significant risk to the health or safety of others that cannot be eliminated by reasonable accommodation.

(4) Employee.—The term "employee" means an individual employed by an employer.

(5) Employer.—

(A) In general.—The term "employer" means a person engaged in an industry affecting commerce who has 15 or more employees for each working day in each of 20 or more calendar weeks in the current or preceding calendar year, and any agent of such person, except that, for two years following the effective date of this title, an employer means a person engaged in an industry affecting commerce who has 25 or more employees for each working day in each of 20 or more calendar weeks in the current or preceding year, and any agent of such person.

(B) Exceptions.—The term "employer" does not include—

(i) the United States, a corporation wholly owned by the government of the United States, or an Indian tribe; or

(ii) a bonafide private membership club (other than a labor organization) that is exempt from taxation under section 501(c) of the Internal Revenue Code of 1986. . . .

(7) Person, etc.—The terms "person," "labor organization," "employment agency," "commerce," and "industry affecting commerce," shall have the same meaning given such terms in section 701 of the Civil Rights Act of 1964 (42 U.S.C. 2000e).

(8) Qualified individual with a disability.—The term "qualified individual with a disability" means an individual with a disability who, with or without reasonable accommodation, can perform the essential functions of the employment position that such individual holds or desires. For the purposes of this title, consideration shall be given to the employer's judgment as to what functions of a job are essential, and if an employer has prepared a written description before advertising or interviewing applicants for the job, this description shall be considered evidence of the essential functions of the job.

(9) Reasonable accommodation.—The term "reasonable accommodation" may include—

(A) making existing facilities used by employees readily accessible to and usable by individuals with disabilities; and

(B) job restructuring, part-time or modified work schedules, reassignment to a vacant position, acquisition or modification of equipment or devices, appropriate adjustment or modifications of examinations, training materials or policies, the provision of qualified readers or interpreters, and other similar accommodations for individuals with disabilities.

(10) Undue Hardship.—

(A) In general.—The term "undue hardship" means an action requiring significant difficulty or expense, when considered in light of the factors set forth in subparagraph (B).

(B) Factors to be considered.—In determining whether an accommodation would impose an undue hardship on a covered entity, factors to be considered include—

(i) the nature and cost of the accommodation needed under this Act;

(ii) the overall financial resources of the facility or facilities involved in the provision of the reasonable accommodation; the number of persons employed at such facility; the effect on expenses and resources, or the impact otherwise of such accommodation upon the operation of the facility;

(iii) the overall financial resources of the covered entity; the overall size of the business of a covered entity with respect to the number of its employees; the number, type, and location of its facilities; and

(iv) the type of operation or operations of the covered entity, including the composition, structure, and functions of the workforce of such entity; the geographic separateness, administrative, or fiscal relationship of the facility or facilities in question to the covered entity.

INDIVIDUALS WITH DISABILITIES EDUCATION ACT (SELECTED PARTS), 20 U.S.C. SECS. 1400–1485

Purpose

It is the purpose of this chapter to assure that all children with disabilities have available to them, within the time periods specified in section 1412(2)(B) of this title, a free appropriate public education which emphasizes special education and related services designed to meet their unique needs, to assure that the rights of children with disabilities and their parents or guardians are protected, to assist States and localities to provide for the education of all children with disabilities, and to assess and assure the effectiveness of efforts to educate children with disabilities.

§ 1401. Definitions

(1) The term "children with disabilities" means children—

(A) with mental retardation, hearing impairments including deafness, speech or language impairments, visual impairments including blindness, serious emotional disturbance, orthopedic impairments, autism, traumatic brain injury, other health impairments, or specific learning disabilities; and

(B) who, by reason thereof need special education and related services. . . .

(15) The term "children with specific learning disabilities" means those children who have a disorder in one or more of the basic psychological processes involved in understanding or in using language, spoken or written, which disorder may manifest itself in imperfect ability to listen, think, speak, read, write, spell, or do mathematical calculations. Such disorders include such conditions as perceptual disabilities, brain injury, minimal brain dysfunction, dyslexia, and developmental aphasia. Such term does not include children who have learning problems which are primarily the result of visual, hearing, or motor disabilities, of mental retardation, of emotional disturbance, or of environmental, cultural, or economic disadvantage.

(16) The term "special education" means specially designed instruction, at no cost to parents or guardians, to meet the unique needs of a child with a disability, including—

(A) instruction conducted in the classroom, in the home, in hospitals and institutions, and in other settings; and

(B) instruction in physical education.

(17) The term "related services" means transportation, and such developmental, corrective, and other supportive services (including speech pathology and audiology, psychological services, physical and occupational therapy, recreation, including therapeutic recreation and social work services, and medical and counseling services, including rehabilitation counseling, except that such medical services shall be for diagnostic and evaluation purposes only) as may be required to assist a child with a disability to benefit from special education, and includes the early identification and assessment of disabling conditions in children.

(18) The term "free appropriate public education" means special education and related services that—

(A) have been provided at public expense, under public supervision and direction, and without charge,

(B) meet the standards of the State educational agency,

(C) include an appropriate preschool, elementary, or secondary school education in the State involved, and

(D) are provided in conformity with the individualized education program required under section 1414(a)(5) of this title.

(19) The term "transition services" means a coordinated set of activities for a student, designed within an outcome-oriented process, which promotes movement from school to post-school activities, including post-secondary education, vocational training, integrated employment (including supported employment), continuing and adult education, adult services, independent living, or community participation. The coordinated set of activities shall be based upon the individual student's needs, taking into account the student's preferences and interests, and shall include instruction, community experiences, the development of employment and other post-school adult living objectives, and, when appropriate, acquisition of daily living skills and functional vocational evaluation.

(20) The term "individualized education program" means a written statement for each child with a disability developed in any meeting by a representative of the local educational agency or an intermediate educational unit who shall be qualified to provide, or supervise the provision of, specially designed instruction to meet the unique needs of children with disabilities, the teacher, the parents or guardian of such child, and, whenever appropriate, such child, which statement shall include—

(A) a statement of the present levels of educational performance of such child,

(B) a statement of annual goals, including short-term instructional objectives,

(C) a statement of the specific educational services to be provided to such child, and the extent to which such child will be able to participate in regular educational programs,

(D) a statement of the needed transition services for students beginning no later than age 16 and annually thereafter (and, when determined appropriate for the individual, beginning at age 14 or younger), including, when appropriate, a statement of the interagency responsibilities or linkages (or both) before the student leaves the school setting.

(E) the projected date for initiation and anticipated duration of such services, and

(F) appropriate objective criteria and evaluation procedures and schedules for determining, on at least an annual basis, whether instructional objectives are being achieved. In the case where a participating agency, other than the educational agency, fails to provide agreed upon services, the educational agency shall reconvene the IEP team to identify alternative strategies to meet the transition objectives.

AGE DISCRIMINATION ACT 29 U.S.C. § 621 (§ 623)

(a) It shall be unlawful for an employer—

(1) to fail or refuse to hire or to discharge any individual or otherwise discriminate against any individual with respect to his compensation, terms, conditions, or privileges of employment, because of such individual's age. . . .

(c) It shall be unlawful for a labor organization—

(1) to exclude or to expel from its membership, or otherwise to discriminate against, any individual because of his age. . . .

(3) to cause or attempt to cause an employer to discriminate against an individual in violation of this section. . . .

(f) It shall not be unlawful for an employer, employment agency, or labor organization—

(1) to take any action otherwise prohibited under subsections (a), (b), (c), or (e) of this section where age is a bona fide occupational qualification reasonably necessary to the normal operation of the particular business, or where the differentiation is based on reasonable factors other than age. . . .

(3) to discharge or otherwise discipline an individual for good cause. . . .

REHABILITATION ACT OF 1973

29 U.S.C. § 794 (§ 504)

The Act provides in part:

"No otherwise qualified handicapped individual . . . shall, solely by reason of his handicap, be excluded from the participation in, be denied the benefits of, or be subjected to discrimination under any program or activity receiving Federal financial assistance."

EQUAL EDUCATION OPPORTUNITIES ACT

20 U.S.C. § 1703

§ 1703 provides:

No State shall deny equal educational opportunity to an individual on account of his or her race, color, sex, or national origin, by—

(a) the deliberate segregation by an educational agency of students on the basis of race, color, or national origin among or within schools. . . .

(c) the assignment by an educational agency of a student to a school, other than the one closest to his or he place of residence within the school district in which he or she resides, if the assignment results in a greater degree of segregation of students on the basis of race, color, sex, or national origin. . . .

(d) discrimination by an educational agency on the basis of race, color, or national origin in the employment, employment conditions, or assignment to schools of its faculty or staff, except to fulfill the purposes of subsection (f) below. . . .

(e) the transfer by an educational agency, whether voluntary or otherwise, of a student from one school to another if the purpose and effect of such transfer is to increase segregation of students on the basis of race, color, or national origin among the schools of such agency; or

(f) the failure by an educational agency to take appropriate action to overcome language barriers that impede equal participation by its students in its instructional programs.

PREGNANCY DISCRIMINATION ACT OF 1978— P.L. 95-555

Be it enacted by the Senate and House of Representatives of the United States of America in Congress assembled, That section 701 of the Civil Rights Act of 1964 is amended by adding at the end thereof the following new subsection:

"(k) The Terms 'because of sex' or 'on the basis of sex' include, but are not limited to, because of or on the basis of pregnancy, childbirth, or related medical conditions; and women affected by pregnancy, childbirth, or related medical conditions shall be treated the same for all employment-related purposes, including the receipt of benefits under fringe benefit programs, as other persons not so affected but similar in their ability or inability to work, and nothing in section 703(h) of this title shall be interpreted to permit otherwise. This subsection shall not require an employer to pay for health insurance benefits for abortion, except where the life of the mother would be endangered if the fetus were carried to term, or except where medical complications have arisen from an abortion: *Provided,* That nothing herein shall preclude an employer from providing abortion benefits or otherwise affect bargaining agreements in regard to abortion."

SEC. 2 (a) Except as provided in subsection (b), the amendment made by this Act shall be effective on the date of enactment.

(b) The provisions of the amendment made by the first section of this Act shall not apply to any fringe benefit program or fund, or insurance program which is in effect on the date of enactment of this Act until 30 days after enactment of this Act.

SEC. 3 Until the expiration of a period of one year from the date of enactment of this Act or, if there is an applicable collective-bargaining agreement in effect on the date of enactment of this Act, until the termination of that agreement, no person who, on the date of enactment of this act is providing either by direct payment or by making contributions to a fringe benefit fund or insurance program, benefits in violation with this act shall, in order to come into compliance with this Act, reduce the benefits or the compensation provided any employee on the date of enactment of this Act, either directly or by failing to provide sufficient contributions to a fringe benefit fund or insurance program: *Provided,* That where the costs of such benefits on the date of enactment of this Act are apportioned between employers and employees, the payments or contributions required to comply with this Act may be made by employers and employees in the same proportion: *And provided further,* That nothing in this section shall prevent the readjustment of benefits or compensation for reasons unrelated to compliance with this Act.

THE FAMILY AND MEDICAL LEAVE ACT OF 1993—PUBLIC LAW 103-3 ENACTED FEBRUARY 5, 1993

An Act

To grant family and temporary medical leave under certain circumstances. Be it enacted by the Senate and House of Representatives of the United States of America in Congress assembled,

Sec. 2. Findings and Purposes.

(a) FINDINGS.—Congress finds that—

(1) the number of single-parent households and two-parent households in which the single parent or both parents work is increasing significantly;

(2) it is important for the development of children and the family unit that fathers and mothers be able to participate in early childrearing and the care of family members who have serious health conditions;

(3) the lack of employment policies to accommodate working parents can force individuals to choose between job security and parenting;

(4) there is inadequate job security for employees who have serious health conditions that prevent them from working for temporary periods;

(5) due to the nature of the roles of men and women in our society, the primary responsibility for family caretaking often falls on women, and such responsibility affects the working lives of women more than it affects the working lives of men; and

(6) employment standards that apply to one gender only have serious potential for encouraging employers to discriminate against employees and applicants for employment who are of that gender.

(b) PURPOSES.—It is the purpose of this Act—

(1) to balance the demands of the workplace with the needs of families, to promote the stability and economic security of families, and to promote national interests in preserving family integrity;

(2) to entitle employees to take reasonable leave for medical reasons, for the birth or adoption of a child, and for the care of a child, spouse, or parent who has a serious health condition;

(3) to accomplish the purposes described in paragraphs (1) and (2) in a manner that accommodates the legitimate interests of employers;

(4) to accomplish the purposes described in paragraphs (1) and (2) in a manner that, consistent with the Equal Protection Clause of the Fourteenth Amendment, minimizes the potential for employment discrimination on the basis of sex by ensuring generally that leave is available for eligible medical reasons (including maternity-related disability) and for compelling family reasons, on a gender-neutral basis; and

(5) to promote the goal of equal employment opportunity for women and men, pursuant to such clause.

Sec. 102. Leave Requirement.

(a) *IN GENERAL.*—

(1) ENTITLEMENT TO LEAVE.—Subject to section 103, an eligible employee shall be entitled to a total of 12 work-weeks of leave during any 12-month period for one or more of the following:

(A) Because of the birth of a son or daughter of the employee and in order to care for such son or daughter.

(B) Because of the placement of a son or daughter with the employee for adoption or foster care.

(C) In order to care for the spouse, or a son, daughter, or parent, of the employee, if such spouse, son, daughter, or parent has a serious health condition.

(D) Because of a serious health condition that makes the employee unable to perform the functions of the position of such employee.

(2) EXPIRATION OF ENTITLEMENT.—The entitlement to leave under subparagraphs (A) and (B) of paragraph (1) for a birth or placement of a son or daughter shall expire at the end of the 12-month period beginning on the date of such birth or placement.

(b) *LEAVE TAKEN INTERMITTENTLY OR ON A REDUCED LEAVE SCHEDULE.*

(1) IN GENERAL.—Leave under subparagraph (A) or (B) of subsection (a)(1) shall not be taken by an employee intermittently or on a reduced leave schedule unless the employee and the employer of the employee agree otherwise. Subject to paragraph (2), subsection (e)(2), and section 103(b)(5), leave under subparagraph (C) or (D) of subsection (a)(1) may be taken intermittently or on a reduced leave schedule when medically necessary. The taking of leave intermittently or on a reduced leave schedule pursuant to this paragraph shall not result in a reduction in the total amount of leave to which the employee is entitled under subsection (a) beyond the amount of leave actually taken.

(2) *ALTERNATIVE POSITION.*—If an employee requests intermittent leave, or leave on a reduced leave schedule, under subparagraph (C) or (D) of subsection (a)(1), that is foreseeable based on planned medical treatment, the employer may require such employee to transfer temporarily to an available alternative position offered by the employer for which the employee is qualified and that—

(A) has equivalent pay and benefits; and

(B) better accommodates recurring periods of leave than the regular employment position of the employee.

(c) *UNPAID LEAVE PERMITTED.*—Except as provided in subsection (d), leave granted under subsection (a) may consist of unpaid leave. Where an employee is otherwise exempt under regulations issued by the Secretary pursuant to section 13(a)(1) of the Fair Labor Standards Act of 1938 (29 U.S.C. 213(a)(1)), the compliance of an employer with this title by providing unpaid leave shall not affect the exempt status of the employee under such section.

(d) *RELATIONSHIP TO PAID LEAVE.*—

(1) UNPAID LEAVE.—If an employer provides paid leave for fewer than 12 workweeks, the additional weeks of leave necessary to attain the 12 workweeks of leave required under this title may be provided without compensation.

(2) SUBSTITUTION OF PAID LEAVE.—

(A) IN GENERAL.—An eligible employee may elect, or an employer may require the employee, to substitute any of the accrued paid vacation leave, personal leave, or family leave of the employee for leave provided under subparagraph (A), (B), or (C) of subsection (a)(1) for any part of the 12-week period of such leave under such subsection.

(B) SERIOUS HEALTH CONDITION.—An eligible employee may elect, or an employer may require the employee, to substitute any of the accrued paid vacation leave, personal leave, or medical or sick leave of the employee for leave provided under subparagraph (C) or (D) of subsection (a)(1) for any part of the 12-week period of such leave under such subsection, except that nothing in this title shall require an employer to provide paid sick leave or paid medical leave in any situation in which such employer would not normally provide any such paid leave.

(e) *FORESEEABLE LEAVE.*—

(1) REQUIREMENT OF NOTICE.—In any case in which the necessity for leave under subparagraph (A) or (B) of subsection (a)(1) is foreseeable based on an expected birth or placement, the employee shall provide the employer with not less than 30 days' notice, before the date the leave is to begin, of the employee's intention to take leave under such subparagraph, except that if the date of the birth or placement requires leave to begin in less than 30 days, the employee shall provide such notice as is practicable.

(2) DUTIES OF EMPLOYEE.—In any case in which the necessity for leave under subparagraph (C) or (D) of subsection (a)(1) is foreseeable based on planned medical treatment, the employee—

(A) shall make a reasonable effort to schedule the treatment so as not to disrupt unduly the operations of the employer, subject to the approval of the health care provider of the employee or the health care provider of the son, daughter, spouse, or parent of the employee, as appropriate; and

(B) shall provide the employer with not less than 30 days' notice, before the date the leave is to begin, of the employee's intention to take leave under such subparagraph, except that if the date of the treatment requires leave to begin in less than 30 days, the employee shall provide such notice as is practicable.

(f) *SPOUSES EMPLOYED BY THE SAME EMPLOYER.*—In any case in which a husband and wife entitled to leave under subsection (a) are employed by the same employer, the aggregate number of workweeks of leave to which both may be entitled may be limited to 12 workweeks during any 12-month period, if such leave is taken—

(1) under subparagraph (A) or (B) of subsection (a)(1); or

(2) to care for a sick parent under subparagraph (C) of such subsection.

APPENDIX

C

Relevant Educational Resources for Teachers and Other Professional Educators

AMERICAN ARBITRATION ASSOCIATION

335 Madison Avenue, Floor 10
New York, NY 10017-4605
Phone: 1-800-778-7879
Fax: 212-716-5907
www.adr.org/index2.1.jsp

Purpose: The American Arbitration Association is available to resolve a wide range of disputes through mediation, arbitration, elections, and other out-of-court settlement procedures. The history, mission, and not-for-profit status of the AAA are unique in the field of alternative dispute resolution. It is, however, the association's ADR resources—its panels, rules, administration, and education and training services—that provide cost-effective and tangible value to counsel, businesses, and industry professionals and their employees, customers, and business partners.

AMERICAN CIVIL LIBERTIES UNION

125 Broad Street, 18th Floor
New York, NY 10004
Phone: 212-549-2500
www.aclu.org/

Purpose: The American Civil Liberties Union (ACLU) is the nation's guardian of liberty. It works daily in courts, legislatures, and communities to defend and preserve the individual rights and liberties guaranteed to every person in this country by the Constitution and laws of the United States. Its job is to conserve America's original civic values—the Constitution and the Bill of Rights.

The American system of government is founded on two counterbalancing principles:

- The majority of the people governs, through democratically elected representatives.
- The power even of a democratic majority must be limited to ensure individual rights.

AMERICAN FEDERATION OF TEACHERS

555 New Jersey Avenue, NW
Washington, DC 20001
Phone: 202-879-4400
www.aft.org/contact.html

Purpose: The mission of the American Federation of Teachers, AFL-CIO, is to improve the lives of its members and their families; to give voice to their legitimate professional, economic, and social aspirations; to strengthen the institutions in which they work; to improve the quality of the services provided; to bring together all members to assist and support one another; and to promote democracy, human rights, and freedom in the union, the nation, and throughout the world.

ASSOCIATION FOR THE SUCCESS OF ALL LEARNERS

1703 N. Beauregard Street
Alexandria, VA 22311
Phone: 9:00 a.m. to 5:00 p.m. eastern time, Monday through Friday
Toll-free from U.S. and Canada: 1-800-933-2723, press 2
Fax: 1-703-575-5400
www.ascd.org/

Purpose: Founded in 1943, the Association for Supervision and Curriculum Development (ASCD) is an international, nonprofit, nonpartisan organization that represents 160,000 educators from more than 135 countries and more than 60 affiliates. Membership spans the entire profession of educators—superintendents, supervisors, principals, teachers, professors of education, and school board members. It is a diverse, international community of educators, forging covenants in teaching and learning for the success of all learners.

The organization addresses all aspects of effective teaching and learning—such as professional development, educational leadership, and capacity building. The ASCD offers broad, multiple perspectives—across all education professions—in reporting key policies and practices. Because it represents all educators, it is able to focus solely on professional practice within the context of "Is it good for the children?" rather than what is reflective of a specific educator role. In short, ASCD reflects the conscience and content of education.

NATIONAL ASSOCIATION OF SECONDARY SCHOOL PRINCIPALS

1904 Association Drive
Reston, VA 20191-1537
Phone: 703-860-0200
www.nassp.org/

Purpose: In existence since 1916, the National Association of Secondary School Principals (NASSP) is the preeminent organization of and national voice for middle school and high school principals, assistant principals, and aspiring school leaders from across the United States and more than 45 countries around the world. The mission of NASSP is to promote excellence in school leadership.

NATIONAL BOARD FOR PROFESSIONAL TEACHING STANDARDS

National Office
1525 Wilson Blvd., Suite 500
Arlington, VA 22209
Phone: 703-465-2700
www.nbpts.org/

Purpose: The National Board for Professional Teaching Standards (NBPTS) is an independent, nonprofit, nonpartisan organization governed by a board of directors, the majority of whom are classroom teachers. Other members include school administrators, school board leaders, governors and state legislators, higher education officials, teacher union leaders, and business and community leaders. It is rooted in the belief that the single-most important action this country can take to improve schools and student learning is to strengthen teaching.

The NBPTS is leading the way in making teaching a profession dedicated to student learning and to upholding high standards for professional performance. It has raised the standards for teachers, strengthened their educational preparation through the standards, and created performance-based assessments that demonstrate accomplished application of the standards. The mission is to advance the quality of teaching and learning by:

- Maintaining high and rigorous standards for what accomplished teachers should know and be able to do
- Providing a national voluntary system certifying teachers who meet these standards
- Advocating related education reforms to integrate National Board Certification in American education and to capitalize on the expertise of National Board Certified Teachers.

NATIONAL COUNCIL ON DISABILITY

1331 F Street, NW, Suite 850
Washington, DC 20004
Phone: 202-272-2004
TTY: 202-272-2074
Fax: 202-272-2022
www.ncd.gov/brochure.htm

Purpose: The National Council on Disability (NCD) was initially established in 1978 as an advisory board within the Department of Education. The council is composed of 15 members, appointed by the President of the United States and confirmed by the U.S. Senate. The Rehabilitation Act Amendments of 1984 transformed NCD into an independent agency.

The overall purpose of the agency is to promote policies, programs, practices, and procedures that guarantee equal opportunity for all people with disabilities, regardless of the nature or severity of the disability, and to empower them to achieve economic self-sufficiency, independent living, and inclusion and integration into all aspects of society.

NATIONAL EDUCATION ASSOCIATION

1201 16th Street, NW
Washington, DC 20036-3290
Phone: Monday–Friday 8:30 a.m.–4:30 p.m. ET 202-833-4000
Fax: 202-822-7974
www.nea.org/

Purpose: To fulfill the promise of a democratic society, the National Education Association promotes the cause of quality public education and advances the profession of education; expands the rights and furthers the interest of educational employees; and advocates human, civil, and economic rights for all.

NATIONAL ASSOCIATION OF ELEMENTARY SCHOOL PRINCIPALS

1615 Duke Street
Alexandria, VA 22314
Phone: 800-386-2377, 703-684-3345
Fax: 800-396-2377
www.naesp.org/

Purpose: The mission of the National Association of Elementary School Principals (NAESP) is to lead in the advocacy and support for elementary and middle school principals and other education leaders in their commitment to all children.

NATIONAL SCHOOL BOARDS ASSOCIATION

1680 Duke Street
Alexandria, VA 22314
Phone: 703-838-6722
Fax: 703-683-7590
E-mail: info@nsba.org
www.nsba.org/site/index.asp

Purpose: The National School Boards Association (NSBA) is a not-for-profit federation of state associations of school boards across the United States. Its mission is to foster excellence and equity in public education through school board leadership. It achieves that mission by representing the school board perspective before federal government agencies and with national organizations that affect education, and by providing vital information and services to state associations of school boards and local school boards throughout the nation.

NO CHILD LEFT BEHIND

U.S. Department of Education
400 Maryland Avenue, SW
Washington, DC 20202
Phone: 1-888-814-NCLB (1-888-814-6252)
TTY: 1-800-437-0833
Fax: 202-401-0689
E-mail: NoChildLeftBehind@ed.gov
www.ed.gov/nclb/landing.jhtml?src=pb

Purpose: The No Child Left Behind Act of 2001 (No Child Left Behind) is a landmark in education reform designed to improve student achievement and change the culture of America's schools. President George W. Bush describes this law as the "cornerstone of his administration."

OFFICE OF HOMELAND SECURITY

The White House
1600 Pennsylvania Avenue NW
Washington, DC 20500
Comments: 202-456-1111
Switchboard: 202-456-1414
FAX: 202-456-2461
E-mail:
President George W. Bush: president@whitehouse.gov
Vice President Richard Cheney: vice.president@
whitehouse.gov
www.whitehouse.gov/homeland/

Purpose: The Department of Homeland Security was created with one single overriding responsibility: to make America more secure. Along with the sweeping transformation within the FBI, the establishment of the Department of Defense's U.S. Northern Command, and the creation of the multi-agency Terrorist Threat Integration Center and Terrorist Screening Center, America is better prepared to prevent, disrupt, and respond to terrorist attacks than ever before.

U.S. DEPARTMENT OF EDUCATION

400 Maryland Avenue, SW
Washington, DC 20202
Telephone: 1-800-USA-LEARN (1-800-872-5327)
TTY: 1-800-437-0833
Fax: 202-401-0689
E-mail: customerservice@inet.ed.gov
www.ed.gov/index.jhtml

Purpose: Congress established the U.S. Department of Education (DOE) on May 4, 1980, in the Department of Education Organization Act (Public Law 96-88 of October 1979). Under this law, DOE's mission is to:

- Strengthen the federal commitment to assuring access to equal educational opportunity for every individual.
- Supplement and complement the efforts of states, the local school systems and other instrumentalities of the states, the private sector, the public and private nonprofit educational research institutions, community-based organizations, parents, and students to improve the quality of education.
- Encourage the increased involvement of the public, parents, and students in federal education programs.
- Promote improvements in the quality and usefulness of education through federally supported research, evaluation, and sharing of information.
- Improve the coordination of federal education programs.
- Improve the management of federal education activities.
- Increase the accountability of federal education programs to the President, the Congress, and the public.

Glossary of Relevant Legal Terms

abatement Termination of a lawsuit.

action A lawsuit proceeding in a court of law.

advisory opinion An opinion generally rendered by a lower court when no actual case is before it.

affidavit A written statement made under oath.

affirm To uphold a lower court's decision or ruling.

allegation A statement in the pleadings of a case that is expected to be proven, usually brought by the plaintiff.

amicus curiae A friend of the court. A party that does not have a direct interest in a case who is requested or offers information to the court to clarify an issue before the court.

appeal An application to a higher court to amend or rectify a lower court's ruling.

appellant One who causes an appeal to a higher court. The appellant may be the plaintiff or the defendant.

appellate court A higher court that hears a case on appeal from a lower court.

appellee A person or party against whom an appeal is brought.

arbitrary An act or action taken without a fair and substantial cause.

assault An offer to use physical force in a hostile manner.

battery Making physical contact with another person in a rude and hostile fashion.

bona fide Acting honestly and in good faith.

breach Failure to execute a legal duty.

brief A written argument presented to a court by attorneys.

case law A body of law created by decisions of the judicial branch.

cause of action The basis for a legal challenge.

certiori A judicial process whereby a case is moved from a lower court to a higher one for review. The record of all proceedings at the lower court is sent to the higher court.

civil action An action in court with the expressed purpose of gaining or recovering individual or civil rights.

civil rights The personal freedoms of citizens guaranteed by the Thirteenth and Fourteenth Amendments to the U.S. Constitution.

class action Legal action brought by one or more individuals on behalf of themselves and others who are affected by a particular issue.

code A systematic compilation of statutes usually arranged into chapters and headings for convenient access.

common law A system of law in which legal principles are derived from usage and custom as expressed by the courts.

compensatory damages Damages awarded to compensate an injured party for actual losses incurred.

complaint A formal plea to a court seeking relief and informing the defendant on the basis for a legal challenge.

concurring opinion An opinion written by a judge expressing the will of the majority in a court ruling.

consent decree Agreement by parties to a dispute and the admission by parties that the decree is a just determination of their rights based on facts related to the case.

contract A legal agreement between parties involving an offer and acceptance to perform certain duties that are enforceable by courts of law.

contributory negligence Negligence by the injured party when combined with the negligence of the defendant resulted in the proximate cause of the injury.

court of record A court that maintains permanent records of its proceedings.

damages Compensation or indemnity claimed by the plaintiff or ordered by the courts for injuries sustained resulting from wrongful acts of the defendant.

declaratory relief An opinion expressed by the court without ordering that anything be done; it recognizes the rights of the parties involved.

decree An order issued by a court in an equity suit.

defamation Scandalous words or expression, written or spoken, that result in damages to another's reputation for which legal action may be taken by the damaged party.

defendant The party against whom a legal action is brought.

deposition A statement of a witness taken under oath obtained before the actual trial.

discretionary power Involves the exercise of judgment in deciding whether to take action in a certain situation.

discrimination The unfair treatment of a group of people by another because of race, gender, religion, culture, or national origin.

dissenting opinion An opinion written by a judge in disagreement with the decision of the majority hearing a case.

due process A course of legal proceedings in accordance with principles of law designed to protect individual rights.

emancipation Legal release from another's control (married child from parents).

enjoin To require an individual by writ of injunction to perform or refrain from a certain act.

felony A crime that is punishable by imprisonment or death.

fiduciary A special relationship between individuals in which one person acts for another in a position of trust.

finding The conclusion reached by a court regarding a factual question.

functional exclusion Disabled students who are provided equal access without special provisions that will enable them to benefit from instruction, although they are physically exposed to the same experience as nondisabled students.

governmental function One that is required of an agency for the protection and welfare of the general public.

hearing An examination of a legal or factual issue by a court.

holding A ruling or decision by the courts on a question or issue properly raised in a case.

implied Inferred; not expressed.

in loco parentis In place of parents.

injunction A court order prohibiting a person from committing an act that threatens or may result in injury to another.

invitee A person who is on the property of another by expressed invitation.

judgment A decision reached by a court.

liable Bound or obligated by law; responsible for actions that may involve restitution.

licensee A person granted the privilege to enter into property by actual or implied consent for his or her own purpose rather than the purpose of the one who owns the property.

litigation Formal challenge involving a dispute in a court; a lawsuit.

malfeasance Commission of an unlawful act.

malice The intentional commission of a wrongful act without justification.

mandate A legal command.

material Important to a case.

ministerial acts Required usually by public officials in which there is no discretion.

misfeasance Improper performance of a lawful act.

motion A request for a court ruling.

negligence A lack of proper care; failure to exercise prudence that may result in injury to another.

nuisance A condition that restricts the use of property or creates a potentially dangerous situation for the user.

original jurisdiction The legal capacity of a court to accept a case at its inception.

parens patriae The state's guardsmanship over those unable to direct their own affairs (e.g., minors).

petition A written application to a court for the redress of a wrong or the grant of a privilege or license.

plaintiff The party who brings action by filing a complaint.

pleadings Formal documents filed in court containing the plaintiff's contention and the defendant's response.

plenary Full; complete.

police powers The inherent power of the government to impose restrictions to protect the health, safety, and welfare of its citizens.

precedent A decision relied on for subsequent decisions in addressing similar or identical questions of law.

prima facie At first view; a fact presumed to be true if not rebutted or proven untrue.

proprietary function Those functions not normally required by statutes or law and usually involving a state or governmental agent.

punitive damages An award intended to punish the wrongdoer.

quid pro quo A consideration; giving one valuable thing in exchange for another.

relief Legal redress sought in the court by the plaintiff.

remand To send back; the act of an appellate court when it sends a case back to the lower court for further proceedings.

remedy A court's enforcement of a right or the prevention of the violation of such right.

respondeat superior The responsibility of a master for the acts of his servants.

respondent The party against whom an appeal is taken; the defendant.

restrain To prevent or prohibit from action.

slander Oral defamation.

sovereign immunity A doctrine providing immunity from suit of a governmental body without its expressed consent.

standing The right to raise an issue in a lawsuit.

stare decisis To stand by a decided case.

statute An act of the state or federal legislative body; a law.

statute of limitations A statute that established the time period in which litigation may be initiated in a particular cause of action.

substantive law The proper law of rights and duties.

suit A proceeding in a court of law initiated by the plaintiff.

summary judgment A court's decision to settle a dispute or dispose of a case promptly without conducting full legal proceedings.

tenure A security measure for those who successfully perform duties and meet statutory or contractual requirements; a continuous service contract.

tort An actionable wrong committed against another independent of contract; a civil wrong.

trespass The unauthorized entry upon the property of another; taking or interfering with the property of another.

vacate To rescind a court decision.

vested Fixed; not subject to any contingency.

vicarious liability A form of liability in which school districts are held liable for negligent or intentional wrongdoing of their employees when the act is committed within the scope of the district employment position, even though the district may not be directly at fault.

void Null; without force or a binding effect.

waiver To forego, renounce, or relinquish a legal right.

warrant A written order of the court; arrest order.

writ of mandamus A command from a court directing a court, officer, or body to perform a certain act.

Index